CHILDREN'S
ENCYCLOPEDIA
OF KNOTS

Barry Mault and William Potter

ARCTURUS

Picture Credits:
Every attempt has been made to clear copyright. Should there be any inadvertent omission, please apply to the publisher for rectification.
Key: b–bottom, t–top, c–center, l–left, r–right

Alamy: 4b (Album), 6t (Art Directors & TRIP), 7bl (Science History Images), 18-19 (Bob Caddick), 32-33 (VPC Photo Collection), 33 (Oleksandr Rupeta), 39 (John Sylvester), 44 (OMG Snap), 46 (Peter Eastland), 52 (Maridav), 54-55 (Craig Steven Thrasher), 54 (Historic Images), 56 (PG Arphexad), 62-63 (Deborah Vernon), 64-65 (Findlay), 66 (Chris Batson), 68-69 (John Morrison), 70tr (piemags), 74-75 (Gary Chapman), 78-79 (Daniel Valla FRPS), 83 (Dorling Kindersley ltd), 84-85 (ULY.U.V), 84 (CHROMORANGE / Bernd Kroeger), 88 (Wirestock, Inc.), 90-91 (dpa picture alliance), 94 (Science History Images),95 (Cavan Images), 96-97 (Bluegreen Pictures), 96 (Cavan Images), 100-101 (Anthony Baker), 100 (Markus Thomenius), 102-103 (Panther Media GmbH), 104-105 (PHOVOIR), 104r (Adrian Muttitt), 106-107 (Glow Asia RF), 108-109 (Jonathan Goldberg), 108 (Julian Lott), 114-115 (neeraj chaturvedi), 118-119 (CBuchananstock), 118t (Gary Eason), 120 (Igor Sarozhkov), 122 (Mike P Shepherd). **Arcturus Picture Library**: all step by step photographs. **Getty**: 6-7 (Holger Leue), 39 (Sepia Times), 76-77 (Andy Sacks). **Shutterstock**: 4-5 (mountainpix), 5t (Abdelrahman Hassanein), 6b (Eowyn_photos), 7br (Yehoshua Halevi), 7t (Andrii Cherniakhov), 8-9 (Tigergallery), 8t (Eric Gomez T), 8b (John Kepchar), 9 (zhukovvvlad), 10-11 (Soraya Plaithong), 12-13 (Africa Studio), 12b (Simon Mayer), 12t (saiko3p), 14-15 (EB Adventure Photography), 14l (r.classen), 14r (sakkmesterke), 16-17 (Damian Hadjiyvanov), 20-21 (Fotokostic), 22-23 (Bapida), 24-25 (lunamarina), 26-27 (PeopleImages.com - Yuri A), 26 (Alvov), 28-29 (Kzenon), Page 28 (Melanie Hobson), 30-31 (Yauhen_D), 32 (sportoakimirka), 34-35 (Iryna Rasko), 36-37 (Dmitry Naumov), 36 (Roman Zaiets), 38-39 (ZADNANE Mohamed), 40-41 (Dainis Derics), 42-43 (Peter Titmuss), 44-45 (Luqman Habibulhaq), 46-47 (pixfly), 48-49 (Elena KA), 48 (Fabio Lamanna), 50-51 (Iryna Inshyna), 52-53 (Tommy Piyatanang), 56-57 (gubernat), 58-59 (Jeanne Provost), 58 (MK photograp55), 60-61 (Viktorus), 60 (Rawpixel.com), 62 (Peter Turner Photography), 64 (Alena Matrosova), 66-67 (CHAINFOTO24), 68 (Predrag Milosavljevic), 70-71 (Kelly vanDellen), 70bl (Sergii Sobolevskyi), 72-73 (Alicia G. Monedero), 72 (david muscroft), 74b (Juice Flair), 78 (Cobalt S-Elinoi), 80-81 (Jorge Salcedo), 80 (ANURAK PONGPATIMET), 82-83 (Vladimir Sukhachev), 86-87 (PedkoAnton), 86 (EJManzaneque), 88-89 (Irene Fox), 90 (Victor Guerrero Diez), 92-93 (Photology1971), 94-95 (kavalenkava), 98-99 (ArtdayAnna), 98 (cosmo.pavone), 99 (Pixel-Shot), 101 (sirtravelalot), 103 (kittisak Moolla), 104l (Ground Picture), 106 (Andrey Piza Stock), 110-111 (Andriy Kananovych), 111 (GBALLGIGGSPHOTO), 112-113 (Inu), 116-117 (gary yim), 116 (MDV Edwards), 117 (Bob Pool), 118b (Krakenimages.com), 120-121 (Victor Velter), 121 (tawanroong), 122-123 (Jaromir Chalabala), 124-125 (Mr. Kosal), 124 (David J. Fred), 125 (Iam_Anuphone). **Wikimedia Commons**: 40 (U. S. Navy), 74t (Georg Fayer).

Jacket all Shutterstock. Front cover: Main image top Denys_Skorikov, bottom New Africa. Top images: l leksiv, cl Susmit Das, c Greg Epperson, cr LightField Studios, r Tibor Duris. Back cover: Evgeny Subbotsky. Front flap: Africa Studio. Back flap: tawanroong.

Authors: Barry Mault and William Potter
Consultant: David Baugh
Editors: Becca Clunes and Rebecca Razo
Designers: Lorraine Inglis and Paul Futcher
Picture research: Lorraine Inglis and Paul Futcher
Design manager: Jessica Holliland
Managing editor: Joe Harris

ISBN: 978-1-3988-5382-9
CH012322US
Supplier 29, Date 0425, PI 00009108

Printed in China

CONTENTS

Introducing Knots

If you've ever tried to untangle a length of string, you probably already know that knots can appear like magic! While it might be frustrating to have a knot forming where you don't want one (like in a stubborn shoelace), knots are very useful and important. They have been used for many purposes, both practical and symbolic, throughout history.

In this book, you will learn all about a variety of knots, binds, hitches, and loops, including their origins and uses, and how to tie them thanks to step-by-step directions and photos. You'll also discover some cool, interesting, and weird knot facts along the way.

The Oldest Rope

The ancient Egyptians are known to have used rope made from papyrus stems—the same plant material they used for making sheets of paper. The oldest piece of Egyptian rope is believed to be 4,000 years old and was probably used on a ship.

This rope from Ancient Egypt dates to around 1550–1295 BCE.

Changing Times

Up until the last century, ropes were usually made from natural fibers, such as cotton or hemp, or other plants. These days, rope is often manufactured from synthetic materials, which are made by humans using chemical processes. Modern ropes made from synthetic nylon have a different texture than rope made from natural fibers. Some knots are less reliable than others in rope or cord made from nylon. This is why it's helpful to know how to create a variety of knots. You'll be able to choose the correct knot for the type of rope and job at hand.

Rope is still sometimes made in the traditional way.

In this carving, ancient Egyptian hunters can be seen carrying rope.

Knot Lingo

Here are some basic terms and definitions to get you started on your journey into the world of knots!

Working end
The end of a rope used to create the knot.

Standing part
The end of a rope (or cord) that isn't used to create a knot. This is also referred to as the hanging part when a rope is suspended from another object.

Bight
A curve in a rope. If the curve is completely closed it becomes a loop.

Loop
A circle in a rope where the ends cross over one another.

Turn to page 126 for a comprehensive glossary of terms.

The Culture of Knots

Knots are essential for many tasks and have been used for thousands of years by sailors, fishers, and animal herders. They have been so important that knots have also been given symbolic meaning throughout history, and some cultures even believe that knots have magical powers.

A decorative knot on a thirteenth-century minaret in Türkiye. Today, this is referred to as a Turk's head knot.

Ceremonial Knots

On the Solomon Islands in the South Pacific, mid-afternoon was once called "the time of the tying of the knot." Knot calendars were used to count down days leading to celebrations. When a chieftain died, 30 knots were tied in a string. These marked the number of new moons that should rise before a funeral feast was arranged.

Medieval Magic

During the Middle Ages, many people believed in knot magic. The witch's knot, consisting of a circle and a four-cornered knot, was carved over the doorways of dwellings to protect inhabitants from evil spirits. These protective knots were also worn as amulets or charms. European lore has it that witches could even bind the wind into knots on a thread. Witches and magicians would sell wind-knots to sailors, who believed they could control the wind at sea by releasing the knots.

A witch's knot

6

Marriage Knots

Knots can represent a union by bringing two cords together. Lovers' knots can be found in many forms across cultural traditions, where a bride and groom are physically attached by a knotted string, or they wear a knot as a symbol of togetherness during the marriage ceremony. In Indian weddings, the couples partake in the tradition of *Granthi Bandhanam*—Sanskrit for "tying of the sacred knot"—in which one end of a cloth is draped over the groom's shoulder and the other end is tied into the bride's sari. This represents the unity of the couple and their families.

Religious Knots

Knots have religious significance, too. They are found in the Jewish tallit, a shawl worn over the shoulders during prayer services. Tied to the four corners of the shawl are knotted fringes called tzitzit, which are said to represent the commandments in the Torah: the Jewish holy book.

The knot has also been found in Islamic art and in mosques.

A sixteenth-century woodcut shows a magician selling a rope with three knots to a merchant captain. Undoing one knot produced a breeze, two knots released a wind, and three knots produced a heavy storm.

The tzitzit knotted fringe

DID YOU KNOW? Each knot has a unique story behind it. Some knots are named for their functions, while others are named for their inventors.

Choosing the Right Knot

When deciding which knot to use for a task, you need to consider two things: strength and security. It's important to know that you can trust the knot to stay tied in place, especially when someone's safety depends on it.

Modern synthetic rope

Friction

Knots depend on friction: a force that slows the movement of two objects sliding, or trying to slide, against each other. Most knots slip a little after pressure is first applied, but once friction takes over, the knots tighten into place. Knots made from natural rope can weaken and fray due to friction; however, modern synthetic rope is more durable, so it's less prone to wear and tear.

Loads

Knots are stronger when the load, or weight, is applied gradually. If the load is applied too quickly—for example, attaching a heavy weight and immediately dropping it from a great height—the rope or cord may break.

Security

Knot security is based on how likely—or unlikely—the ropes or cords are to stay in place when they are tied in a knot.

Consider the Material

Some knots might slip more easily than others depending on the material they are tied into, which is why it's important to select the correct knot for the job. Fishing line, for example, is made from sleek, slippery material, so it requires a fisherman's knot (see page 28) or one specifically created for fishing line.

Always check the security of a knot before putting it to use.

Tightening the Knot

One of the most important factors in knot security is making sure the knot is properly tightened. Always take a few moments to check. The more complex the knot, the more important this is.

Chapter 1

Basic Knots

This chapter covers several basic knots that are perfect for beginning knot enthusiasts. These are the overhand knot, the figure 8 knot, and Ashley's stopper knot, for those occasions when you need a thick knot that won't slip through a hole. You will also find two basic knots for stopping the ends of a rope from fraying: the common whipping knot and the West Country whipping knot. Once you master the knots in this chapter, you'll be well on your way to building your skills as an expert knottologist!

Knot in Use

Here's a quick glance at the knots in this chapter and some of their uses.

Overhand Knot: Used for practical purposes, such as tying string to a package.

Figure 8 Knot: Often used as a stopping knot.

Common Whipping Knot: Used for preventing the ends of a rope from fraying.

West Country Whipping Knot: Also used to prevent fraying, but this one is easier to learn.

Ashley's Stopper Knot: Used for stopping rope from sliding through a hole or an opening.

Practice Makes a Perfect Knot

You don't need fancy rope to practice tying knots. String, a length of yarn, or an old shoelace are perfect for learning. Knots need to be strong and secure when you're using them for real tasks, but try not to tighten your practice knots too much—you'll want to be able to untie them while you continue to improve your skills.

Overhand Knot

The overhand knot is the simplest of knots, and you probably already know how to tie it. While it's an easy knot to remember, it's a weaker knot that can be difficult to untie, so it has limited uses. It's often used as the first step in tying other knots.

Inca Communication

One of the most interesting places an overhand knot can be seen is on a quipu (pronounced "kee-poo"): a series of knotted strings descending from a horizontal cord. Quipus were used by the Incan Empire which ruled much of western South America from the fifteenth to the sixteenth century. Instead of writing, the Inca used quipus for sharing information. The quipu featured single and multiple overhand knots and figure 8 knots (see page 14).

The Inca built many temples, citadels, and cities, including Machu Picchu in Peru.

Quipu Cords

Most Inca worked as farmers, growing crops and raising alpacas and llamas. Llama wool was dyed, spun, and used for clothing and for making quipus. Quipucamayocs, or knot keepers, had the job of tying knots on quipus. This system of knotted strings was used in South America for thousands of years.

The different knots in a quipu represented numbers in a decimal system. A gap stood for a zero. The position of the knots on each string could also change their value.

1

Start with the cord laid out as shown.

2

Take the working end back, over the standing part. Pass the working end up through the loop formed, then pull the ends to tighten.

To secure a balloon, start with an overhand knot. Wrap both ends of string around the base two more times. Make another overhand knot, then double knot it.

DID YOU KNOW? Some of the largest quipus include as many as 1,500 knotted strings along their length.

Figure 8 Knot

If the overhand knot is too small or too insecure for your purposes, try using the figure 8 knot, which is slightly thicker and easier to untie. The figure 8 is a type of stopper knot, which stops a rope from slipping through a hole or an opening.

Dough Knots?

A pretzel loop resembles the figure 8 knot, although this chewy snack isn't a knot at all! This tasty bread is thought to have been invented in the Middle Ages, possibly by European monks as a reward for children learning their prayers. The "knot" in the dough is more of a twist and may represent arms crossing the chest. The pretzel is rolled into a long tube shape, and then its ends are folded over one another twice to form a loop. The free ends are then pressed into to the top of the loop before baking. To learn more about real loop knots, turn to page 82.

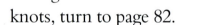

Before it is baked, the pretzel dough is shaped into a knot called a loop or bow.

DID YOU KNOW? The word "pretzel" may come from the Latin *brachiatus* meaning it has branches like arms.

The figure 8 knot makes for a good stopper knot to create a rope handle on a bucket.

A stopper knot creates a thick end on a rope. It stops the rope from slipping through a hole.

Start as if you are going to tie an overhand knot but with the end taken back and over the standing part. Take the end under the standing part to form the figure 8 and through the original loop.

Common Whipping Knot

Whipping knots are generally used to prevent the ends of a rope from fraying; however, they can also be used for decorative purposes, such as to create tassels.

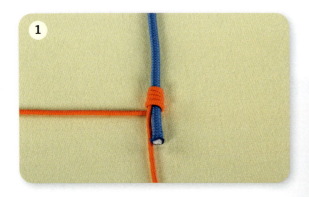

1

Lay the end of the twine (shown in orange) along the rope with the end of the twine extending well beyond the rope's end. Now wrap the twine tightly about five times around the rope and the twine itself, working toward the end of the rope.

2

Bring the protruding end of the twine back to form a bight (curve) and continue to wrap twine tightly over the legs of the bight, leaving a loop emerging from under the wraps.

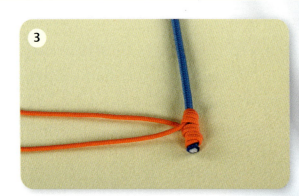

3

Tuck the working end of the twine through the loop formed at the end and tug sharply on the end of the loop, which will pull the working end back under its own wraps, trapping it.

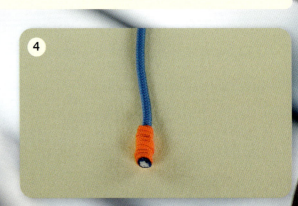

4

Trim off the ends to complete the whipping.

Knots need to withstand movements like jerking, shaking, and pulling. This is why preventing fraying is so important. Always check that your knot is secure before putting it into practice.

To prevent fraying, some modern ropes feature a plastic or rubber shrink wrap over each end.

DID YOU KNOW? All ropes and cords will fray at their ends eventually unless steps are taken to prevent it. You can buy ready-made waxed whipping twine to help reinforce your whipping knots so they are sturdier at the ends.

West Country Whipping Knot

This slightly bulky whipping knot is sturdy and works well with heavier rope. This style of whipping is not common, but when it's done correctly, it is neat and secure.

Sealing a rope with tape provides a temporary fix until you can permanently stop the rope from fraying with a whipping knot.

Tape Trick

Whipping knots are often used to prevent fraying after a rope has been cut. If you do need to shorten a rope, there are simple steps you can take to keep the cut as neat as possible. Wrap plastic electrician's tape several times around the rope, right at the point where you want to cut. This provides a quick way to "seal" the end. Next, ask an adult to use a sharp knife to cut through the taped part of the rope. When the cut has been made, remove the tape and use a whipping knot to prevent fraying permanently.

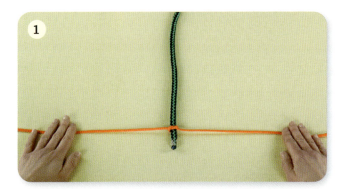

Place the center of the whipping twine beneath the end of the rope, and tie an overhand knot tightly on top of the rope.

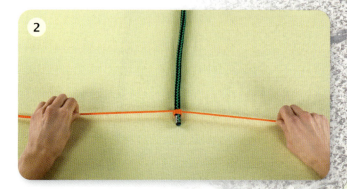

Wrap the twine around the back of the rope as you pull it into another overhand knot. Bring the twine back to the front and repeat.

DID YOU KNOW? It's likely that the West Country whipping knot took its name from England's "West Country." This coastal region is known for its maritime and seafaring activities.

3

Thicker cord has been used here for demonstration purposes.

Continue Step 2 several times until the whipping is at the length desired. If the twine is not waxed, you can add a drop of liquid glue to the ends to seal them in place.

Ashley's Stopper Knot

Have you ever tied a knot at the end of a thread to sew a button onto a garment? That little knot prevents the thread from coming all the way through the fabric. This is called a stopper knot. In the early twentieth century, American knot expert Clifford Ashley introduced the thick, tight stopper knot that bears his name. Stopper knots can be big or small depending on the opening of the hole.

Knot Collector

This stopper knot is especially good for use with outdoor play equipment, such as swings. However, Clifford Ashley originally became interested in the knots used in sailing. Ashley, an artist, began drawing the knots used by sailors and organized them into one encyclopedia. Published in 1944 and updated many times since, *The Ashley Book of Knots* is considered the definitive reference book of knots. It features 7,000 drawings of knots and tools.

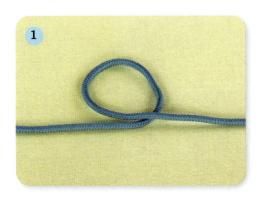

Start with the cord laid out as shown.

Bend the cord to create a bight, or curve, to the right of the loop. Pull it through the loop as shown. This creates a slip knot. Tighten the knot around the neck of the loop by pulling on the standing part.

Rotate the rope 90° clockwise. Tuck the working end through the loop from the back as shown.

Swings require thick ropes to support the body weight of the user. Also, the thicker the rope, the easier it is to hold on to.

Tie this stopper knot on the ends of a rope going through a swing seat, especially if the seat holes are large.

4

Tighten the loop to trap the working end by pulling on the standing part.

5

Pull the working end to finish the knot.

DID YOU KNOW? Clifford Ashley studied knots for over 40 years. It took him 11 years to write his encyclopedia, which is still in print today.

Chapter 2

Bends

Bends are knots that join two or more ropes together to make one longer rope. Choosing the right bend is important when the ropes being joined are made of different materials or are different thicknesses—this is because they are more likely to slip or come undone. As always, remember to check that your knots are securely in place before putting them to work!

The Bends

Here's a quick look at the bends in this chapter.

Albright Knot: Used for joining two fishing lines of varying weights or for catching heavy fish.

Carrick Bend: Used to join heavy-duty rope or cord.

Fisherman's Knot: Generally used for fishing.

Hunter's Bend: Often used for towing a heavy load.

Sheet Bend: Useful for temporary fixes, such as a broken shoelace.

Double Slipped Sheet Bend: Useful for tethering animals or securing loads.

Water Knot: Used to join flat bands, straps, or cords.

Lapp Knot: Used to secure bundles, often in snowy conditions.

Zeppelin Bend: Once used to tether airships to mooring masts.

Coming Undone

When choosing a bend knot, think carefully about whether you will need to untie the ropes again. The zeppelin bend (see page 40) can be untied easily, but the fisherman's knot (see page 28) is almost impossible to undo!

Albright Knot

Jimmie Albright, well known in America in the twentieth century as a fishing guide, created the Albright knot—also known as the Albright special and the Alberto knot—to join a heavier type of fishing leader line to a lighter main fishing line for the purpose of catching big, heavy fish like tarpon.

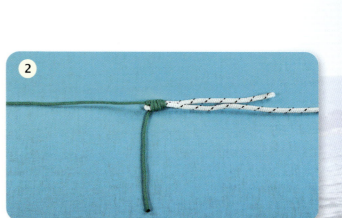

Captain Albright was a guide known for taking wealthy and famous people on fishing trips around the Florida Keys in the USA.

A Tangle of Names

Like the Albright knot, many knots have more than one name. A single knot may have different names depending on its intended use. For example, the clove hitch (see page 56) has many uses, so it has many names. It's also known as the boatman's hitch, the builder's knot, and the steamboat hitch. Like the Albright knot, there are knots named after the people credited with inventing them, such as the Prusik knot (see page 74).

1

Make a bight, or curve, at the end of the thicker material (rope). Lay the thinner material (string) over the bight, and wrap it around the rope as shown.

2

Continue to wrap the string tightly around the rope toward the bight, trapping the horizontal length of string as you work. After you have wrapped the string around the rope four or five times, thread the working end of the string down through the bight of the rope.

An Albright knot is one of many knots used for fishing. It is used to attach fine nylon thread to thicker line.

The number of wraps used on an Albright knot corresponds to the pound capacity of the fishing line. A line that can hold fewer pounds requires more wraps; a line that can hold more pounds requires fewer wraps.

3

Slide the string to the end of the bight and pull on both ends to tighten.

DID YOU KNOW? Tarpon are nicknamed "silver king," due to their size and shiny scales. They can grow up to 8 ft (2.4 m) and can weigh nearly 300 lb (136 kg)!

Carrick Bend

The carrick bend is used to join two thick or heavy-duty ropes together. In fact, it's considered one of the best bends for pulling heavy loads, which is why it's perfect for connecting large ropes used in a tug-of-war game.

All at Sea

The carrick bend is a secure knot that is reliable even under slick or wet conditions—another reason it works for a tug-of-war, which often takes place over a mud puddle. It was originally used to join thick, oversized towing or mooring ropes aboard ships. Even under a heavy load, it can be worked loose and untied.

The carrick bend is just one of hundreds of knots that were used aboard ships at sea. The two half hitches (see page 46) and the bowline (see page 90) were used with heavy-duty ropes to moor ships. Over the years, however, many of these knots, including the carrick, have been adapted for use on land and have proved their usefulness many times over.

Lay the first rope (shown in white) horizontally. Then create a loop as shown above. Lay the second rope (shown in red) underneath the loop of the first rope, with the working end to the left.

Reposition the working end of the first rope so it is pointing downward. Now, take the working end of the second rope down and over the standing part of the first rope. Continue to thread the second rope in an under-over-under-over sequence, as shown. The second rope finishes with the working end on top of the loop of the first rope.

The carrick bend is a strong knot. It's useful for joining ropes of similar thickness together—perfect for a tug-of-war match!

3

Tighten the knot by pulling on both working ends. Your finished knot should look like this.

DID YOU KNOW? In 2005, a rope with a diameter of 2.2 m (7 ft 2 in) was made out of rice straw for a tug-of-war competition in Uiryeonggun, South Korea. It was the largest rope ever made from natural materials.

Fisherman's Knot

The fisherman's knot is a reliable knot originally used by anglers (someone who fishes with a rod and line) to repair a broken fishing line. Once it's pulled together and tightened, this knot is strong, secure, and almost impossible to undo, making it great for catching fish! It's the perfect knot for ropes or lines that need to be permanently joined.

Catch of the Day

The fisherman's knot has several other names, including the angler's knot, the halibut knot, and the true lovers' knot! In addition to using bends like the fisherman's knot, fishers frequently use hitches (see page 42) for a variety of purposes. Fishers who specialize in catching crab, lobster, and eel often use the ground line hitch (see page 64) to connect anchors, buoys, and nets to their pots.

Lobster pots have a small opening so lobsters can enter but cannot escape. The pots are baited and dropped to the seafloor. They are attached to a buoy with a rope and knot so they can found again.

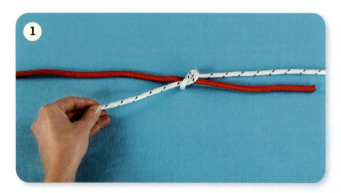

1

Lay the two ropes side by side, with the working ends facing in opposite directions. Take one of the ropes and tie its working end in an overhand knot (see page 12) around the other rope, as shown.

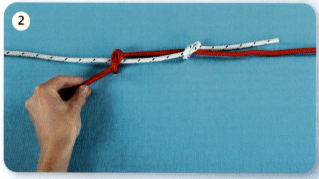

2

Repeat Step 1 with the length of rope that doesn't already have a knot in it, by tying its working end around the standing part of the other rope.

DID YOU KNOW? There are about 200 known fishing knots. Many of these are similar knots with minor alterations between them. Most people use anywhere from two to six knots for fishing.

The fisherman's knot is useful for tying lengths of fishing line together.

3

Tighten each overhand knot individually, and then pull on the standing parts so the knots slide together and lock.

Hunter's Bend

The hunter's bend is made up of two interlocked overhand knots (see page 12). It is a strong and reliable knot to use when joining two ropes or cords, but sometimes it can jam when it's pulled too tightly, making it difficult to undo.

Knot Tyers United

Inspired by a press report announcing the invention of a new knot—the hunter's bend—a group of knot enthusiasts formed the International Guild of Knot Tyers (IGKT) in 1982. For anyone with a serious interest in knotting, this organization aims to preserve traditional knotting techniques, consult on new knotting methods, and promote the art, practice, and use of knots. The guild was formed in the United Kingdom, but it now has branches in France, Germany, the Netherlands, Sweden, North America, and New Zealand. Anyone with an interest in knotting can join!

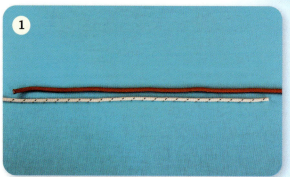

1. Lay the two cords side by side, with the working ends in opposite directions, as shown.

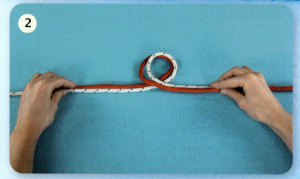

2. Take hold of both cords to the right of the middle and fold them over to the left to form a pair of loops.

DID YOU KNOW? The Six Knot Challenge is an event hosted by the IGKT. Competitors race against the clock to tie six basic knots. The current record holder completed the challenge in 8.1 seconds.

The hunter's bend was a minor sensation when it was introduced in 1978 because it was the "world's first new knot in 20 years," according to newspaper reports. Its creator, Dr. Edward Hunter, became a bit of a celebrity in the knot world.

The hunter's bend is often used with a tow rope thanks to its durability and reliablity.

3

The loop in the white cord now sits on top and the loop in the red cord sits underneath. Take the working end of the top (white) cord and thread it up through the middle of both loops.

4

Take the working end of the red cord and lead it up through the loop. Then take it down behind the standing part of the white cord as shown. The working end of the white cord should still point up.

5

Pull both standing parts to tighten the knot.

Sheet Bend

An old sailor's knot, the sheet bend can be used to tie two lengths of rope together. It is not a very secure or strong knot, so it's best suited to tasks like fixing a broken lace or joining ropes to set up a tent. The double sheet bend (see opposite page) adds extra security, especially if the two ropes being joined are different thicknesses.

Scouts' Honor

The sheet bend is one of several knots taught to scouts. Established in 1907, the Scout Movement's aim is to encourage young people to particpate in outdoor activities, such as camping, hiking, and woodcrafting, as well as master various skills, including knot making.

Scout neckerchiefs are traditionally held in place with a sliding leather ring called a woggle, but they can also be tied with a decorative knot and exchanged with fellow scouts at international gatherings like the World Scout Jamboree.

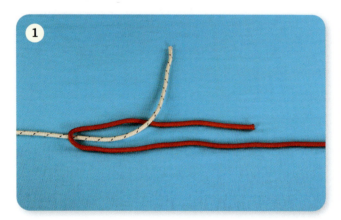

1 Make a bight in the end of the first rope (the thicker one, if they are of different thicknesses). Thread the working end of the second rope through the bight of the first rope, as shown.

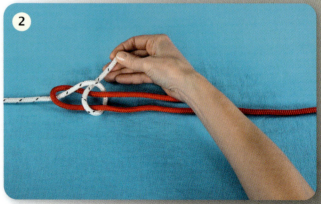

2 Now bring the working end of the second rope down behind the bight, then up across the front, tucking it under itself. Pull the ends to tighten.

DID YOU KNOW? The Scout Association is the largest youth organization in the world, with 57 million Scouts and volunteers in 176 countries.

Use the sheet bend as a quick fix for frayed or broken shoelaces. Lengthen your laces by simply tying on an extra piece of string.

3

Double Sheet Bend
For a stronger knot, wrap the second rope around the bight twice before tucking it under itself and tightening.

The sheet bend is one of six or seven basic knots that Scouts must learn to earn their Pioneer Activity or Pioneering Merit Badge.

Double Slipped Sheet Bend

This knot is useful because it is strong, but it can be undone quickly by pulling on its end. It is similar to the sheet bend (see page 32), but it is wrapped around its connecting rope twice, instead of once. It's another knot that is effective for securing ropes of different diameters and sizes.

March of the Camels

The double slipped sheet bend is another multipurpose knot often used for sailing and camping, as well as for tethering animals to each other or to a post. In fact, this bend might have been used in so-called desert or camel caravans thousands of years ago to transport goods and people across the deserts of Asia and Africa.

Knot Alternative

The rolling hitch (see page 76), is another useful knot for tethering animals for the same reasons as the double slipped sheet bend. It is secure, easy to adjust, and unties quickly in an emergency.

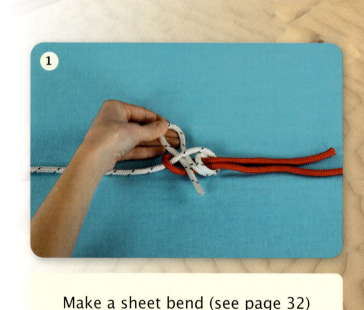

1

Make a sheet bend (see page 32) but instead of tucking the end of the second rope under itself, make it into a bight and tuck it under itself, as shown. This is your quick release cord!

2

The double slipped sheet bend is a good knot to tether lines of animals. The knot can be released quickly, if necessary.

Tighten the knot by pulling the ends of the ropes. To turn the knot into a regular sheet bend, pull the working end of the slipped sheet bend.

DID YOU KNOW? Ancient Egyptians used fibers from date palms, the stalks of plant flax, papyrus, leather, and even camel hair to make rope.

Water Knot

The water knot is a bend especially designed to join flat synthetic material, such as two straps or tapes. It can also be used to fix a broken strap. For extra security, each end should be tied in a stopper knot (see page 20).

Knotty Nylon

Slacklines are often made from nylon. Nylon was invented in the 1930s and was used during World War II in parachute cords and ropes for towing gliders. Following this, it began to be used for towing and mooring boats, and then by climbers in the 1940s. Synthetic fibers allowed a greater variety of rope shapes to be manufactured, including flat straps. One drawback of nylon is that the rope can be slippery compared to rope made from natural fibers, causing the cords to unravel.

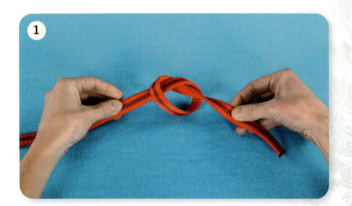

Tie a loose overhand knot (see page 12) near to the working end of the first strap.

Now take the second strap and thread its working end back through the overhand knot. Trace the path of the first strap until the working end of the second strap emerges alongside the standing part of the first strap. If the knot is going to be used with a heavy load, make sure that the two working ends are at least several inches long.

In slacklining, a person walks across a length of webbing that is suspended low to the ground.

The rope used for slacklining is usually flat, making the water knot an ideal choice if the line needs to be tied.

3

Tighten the knot carefully.

DID YOU KNOW? In Germany, the water knot also has the unfortunate name *todesknoten*, meaning "death knot"—although it is no more dangerous than any other knot when used correctly.

Lapp Knot

This relative of the sheet bend (see page 32) has been used by the Sámi people for a long time. The Sámi are native to Norway, Sweden, Finland, and Russia in an area formally known as Lapland—hence the name of the knot.

Rope for Cold, Snowy Conditions

The Lapp knot is easy to create, which is good news for cold fingers! This may explain its popularity with the Sámi. The Lapp knot is frequently used to secure bundles or packages. With one pull, it releases easily, making it useful for getting things untied quickly—perfect when it's too cold outside to fiddle with it! Today, the Sámi often use synthetic rope. These ropes are generally stronger than natural fibers, and they are more resistant to rotting. This is a useful property in situations where a rope is exposed to snow or rain.

Pay attention to the direction of the ends when tying the Lapp knot—both standing parts need to be on the same side of the knot.

To prevent the rope from slipping or coming undone, tie this knot to a secure loop knot, such as an angler's loop (see page 88) or a common bowline (see page 90).

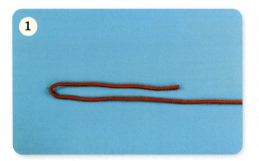

Take the end of the first rope and fold it back to form a bight, like this.

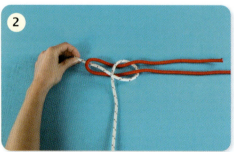

Feed the working end of the second rope over and around the bight. Then take the working end back across itself and tuck it through the bight of the first rope. Pull the ends to tighten.

Slipped Lapp Knot
Create a Lapp knot, as above. Before tightening, make a bight in the second rope by feeding the working end back through the bight of the first rope.

DID YOU KNOW? The Sámi people traditionally used knots on a string called a "wind rope" to try to control the weather.

Reindeer were traditionally used by the Sámi people to pull sleds, and the Lapp knot was used in the harnessing.

A traditional Sámi sled resembles a canoe. It is known as an ackja.

Many Sámi people still herd reindeer today, although snowmobiles are more common than sleds.

Zeppelin Bend

This knot gets its name because it was used to tie down large airships, known as zeppelins. The knot is made up of two interlocked overhand knots, and it can be used to join ropes of different sizes and materials. It is a very secure knot that is easy to undo and is therefore considered one of the best bends to use for a number of tasks.

Charles Rosendahl, who popularized the zeppelin bend, began his Navy career as the commanding officer on the airship USS *Los Angeles*. Here it is seen at the mooring mast on the USS *Patoka*.

Airship Tethers

Zeppelins were used to protect cargo ships on the ocean during World War I. They had a rigid outer body filled with hydrogen and a gondola, or passenger carriage, underneath for the crew. Zeppelins docked at mooring masts, which had a platform where the crew could disembark. The zeppelin bend—also known as the Rosendahl bend after US Navy officer Charles Rosendahl—was considered particularly suitable for tethering these large airships. Rosendahl demanded this knot be used for attaching the airships under his command.

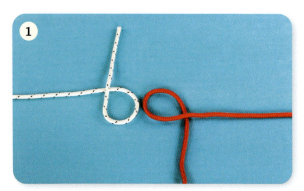

1

Create a "b" shape with one rope, and a "q" shape with the other. Make sure the working end of the "b" shape is on top of the standing part, and the working end of the "q" shape is underneath the standing part.

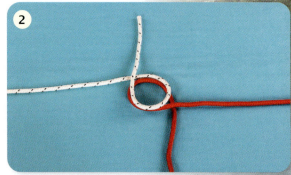

2

Place the "b" on top of the "q."

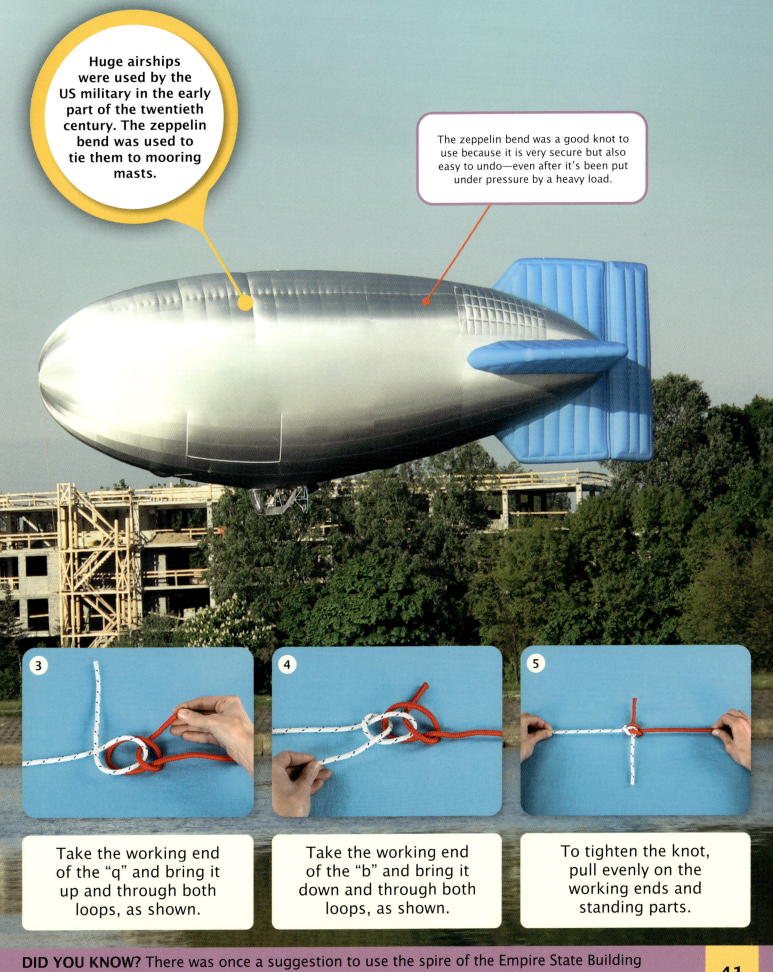

Huge airships were used by the US military in the early part of the twentieth century. The zeppelin bend was used to tie them to mooring masts.

The zeppelin bend was a good knot to use because it is very secure but also easy to undo—even after it's been put under pressure by a heavy load.

3

Take the working end of the "q" and bring it up and through both loops, as shown.

4

Take the working end of the "b" and bring it down and through both loops, as shown.

5

To tighten the knot, pull evenly on the working ends and standing parts.

DID YOU KNOW? There was once a suggestion to use the spire of the Empire State Building in New York as a mooring mast for airships, although it was never used for this purpose.

Chapter 3

Hitches

A hitch is a type of knot that is used to attach a rope or cord to another object—oftentimes, another rope. Some hitches attach a rope to a pole, a post, or other stationary support. Hitch knots can be moved easily by sliding them along the support object, but they will grip once pulled on tightly.

Getting Hitched

Here's a quick glance at the hitch knots in this chapter.

Half Hitch, Knute Hitch, Tensionless Hitch: Often used to hang items.

Round Turn & Two Half Hitches: Perfect for securing tarps in place.

Anchor Hitch: A great knot for creating a rope swing.

Becket Hitch: Used to join a rope line to a loop.

Blake's Hitch, Clove Hitch, Prusik Knot: Used for climbing.

Buntline Hitch: A knot used to tie sails.

Cow Hitch: Created to tether cows to a pole for grazing.

Highwayman's Hitch: An easy knot with quick release.

Gnat Hitch: A small knot used to secure lightweight things.

Ground Line Hitch: A fishing knot for securing pots and nets.

Pipe Hitch, Rolling Hitch, Timber Hitch: Construction and lumber knots to move large pipes or tree branches.

Knute Hitch, Marlinspike Hitch: Often used to create a handle.

Pile Hitch and Double Pile Hitch: A great hitch for mooring boats.

Half Hitch

The half hitch is similar to the overhand knot, in a sense, because it isn't a secure knot on its own. It's often used as a first step in a process using other knots, such as the round turn & two half hitches (see page 46) or a buntline hitch (see page 54).

Carpenter's Knots

The half hitch is one of many knots used in olden times by carpenters, particularly for suspending tools or even timber from a pole or a frame. Other knots used by carpenters included the clove hitch (see page 56) for hanging a hammer or other tools, and the timber hitch (see page 80) for hoisting boards. The half hitch has practical functions, but for it to be reliable, it must be used with other knots, bends, or hitches to perform a task.

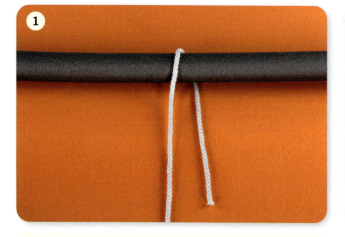

1	Take the working end of the rope over the object and around to the right of the standing part.

2 The working end now goes around the standing part, forming the half hitch.

DID YOU KNOW? Carpenters invented a 3D puzzle made from six interlocking pieces of wood with notches that fit together, which they called the Devil's knot. When assembled correctly, the pieces create a small, compact cross.

Yokes, used for carrying loads of equal weight distribution, have been used for thousands of years. Farmers used yokes for carrying buckets of water, as well as to connect horses or cattle to a plow.

The half hitch can be used in conjunction with a buntline hitch to suspend jerry cans from a carrying pole for transport.

Round Turn & Two Half Hitches

While its name is a mouthful, each part actually describes exactly how this hitch should be tied. That makes it easy to remember! This strong, reliable knot contains an extra loop over a support rail or other object, which means that some of its load is taken up by friction, which adds extra security. Loosen the knot slightly, and you will see that the free end is actually a clove hitch (see page 56).

Perfect in a Pinch

Need to hang a clothesline while you're camping in the woods or at the beach? This hitch has you covered. Simply tie the hitch on a tree and pull the line taut, then repeat the hitch on another tree nearby to secure it in place. It's perfect for air drying clothes, socks, and sleeping bags.

Take a complete turn (known as a round turn) around the rail, or whatever the hitch is to be attached to, leading to the right.

Tie a half hitch around the standing part.

DID YOU KNOW? It's possible that tying a rope to make a clothesline is a relatively recent activity. The word *clothesline* dates to the year 1830. Prior to the invention of the clothesline, people dried their garments by laying them on rocks.

A round turn & two half hitches can be used to attach a rope to a tent ring, for extra stability in bad weather.

3 Repeat Step 2, tying a second half hitch below the first one. Both half hitches should be the same, with the working end emerging to the right.

4 Tighten by first pulling on the working end and the standing part to slide the knot up to the attachment point.

Anchor Hitch

Also known as the fisherman's bend, this knot is actually a hitch, which might sound confusing! The old name probably originated from sailors "bending a rope" onto or around something, such as a post or rail. This hitch is more secure than a round turn & two half hitches (see page 46), and it can be used to secure a small boat anchor—just like its name suggests.

Swing Time

People have been enjoying swings for thousands of years, and the rope may well have been secured with an anchor hitch. Swings date back to ancient Egypt and are seen in artwork from the fifth century and later. In the eighteenth century, the swing was used as a cure for fevers, gout, and even seasickness. Even if rocking back and forth has little effect on illness, there's no denying that time spent on a swing is something fun that often makes you feel better.

This hitch is great for tying down luggage or camping gear on a roof rack under a tarp.

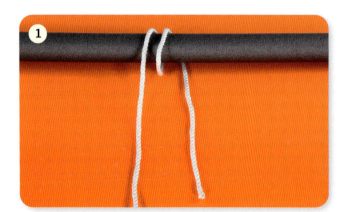

Make a complete turn around the ring or bar with the working end of the rope.

Take the working end over the standing part and lead it under the round turns that are wrapped around the ring or bar. This makes a half hitch secured by these two turns.

The anchor hitch can be used to attach a rope swing to a horizontal tree branch.

3

Use the working end to make a half hitch around the standing part. Tighten and make sure the knot is pressed close to the attachment point.

4

Alternate method: Instead of Step 3, repeat Step 2 and take a second turn under the round turns.

DID YOU KNOW? Ships with anchors date back thousands of years. The first anchors were added to ships built between 5000 and 6000 BCE in ancient Egypt.

Becket Hitch

A becket hitch is similar to the sheet bend (see page 32), but rather than joining the ends of two lines, it is used to join a line to a loop. If the ropes are different types or sizes, a becket hitch can be doubled for a more secure attachment. Using a becket hitch with a poacher's knot (see page 108) is a secure way to hang a tarp or a hammock.

Hanging Around

Hammocks have been used in Central America for over 1,000 years. They keep sleepers off the ground, away from biting insects, snakes, and other dangerous creatures. Hammocks were also popular on board European ships in the sixteenth century. A hammock sways with the movement of the ship, making it less likely that a sleeping sailor will be tipped out in rough weather.

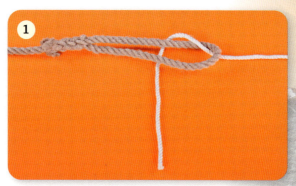

Lead the working end up through the loop and around the back of the loop.

Take the working end back over the loop and under itself. If the knot is to be doubled, then repeat this step. A back-up overhand knot tied in the working end will add some security against slippage.

DID YOU KNOW? Some South American cultures refer to the becket hitch as the hammock knot.

A becket hitch can be used to attach hammock strings to the loops in your support cords or ropes.

You can also use a becket hitch to join a cord to the sling on a tool handle, so you can carry it over your shoulder.

3

Pass the working end up through the loop, around the back of both loop legs and over and down through the loop again. At this point, the two ropes have the appearance of a reef knot.

4

Lead the working end underneath the standing part and thread under its loop legs. Work tight.

5

The knot after tightening.

Blake's Hitch

This hitch is named after arborist, or tree specialist, James Blake. Blake first demonstrated this knot to other arborists in 1994, and it became a popular knot to use when ascending and descending trees. The cord used to make this hitch is thinner than the rope it is tied to so that it can slide along the support line with ease.

Branch Line

If you enjoy climbing trees, perhaps arborist is the career for you. Arborists, also called tree surgeons, look after the health and safety of individual trees. This often involves using ropes to climb up trees and inspect them for disease or damage that may cause large branches or even the whole tree to fall. Arborists may recommend trimming branches, removing deadwood, or cutting down trees completely. It's a job that definitely has its ups and downs.

A Blake's hitch can also provide a heavy-duty adjustable loop for a tent's guy line.

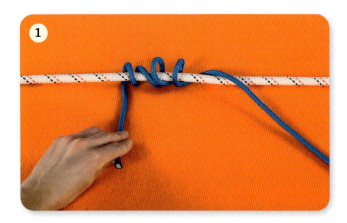

With the working end of a thinner rope, make four turns around the thicker rope in the opposite direction to the pull. The first two turns should be kept loose, so tying these around the thumb can be helpful.

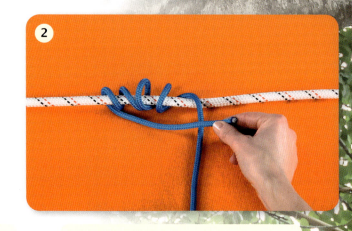

With the working end emerging from behind the rope, bring it down and over the standing part.

DID YOU KNOW? There are thought to be 73,000 species of tree in the world, including about 9,200 still to be identified!

Tree workers use this hitch as a "slide-and-grip" knot, which allows for easy but secure movement.

3

Now tuck the working end under the first two turns around the back of the main rope.

4

Tighten all parts carefully before use. If this knot is being used in a dangerous situation, add an overhand or figure 8 knot to the working end to prevent it pulling out if the knot twists.

Buntline Hitch

A buntline is a vertical rope used to pull a sail up. The buntline hitch is an old sailing knot originally used to tie the square sail to its buntlines. As strong winds flapped the sails, the knot would conveniently tighten rather than loosen, making it even more secure. The downside of the buntline hitch is that it can jam under a heavy load.

Prince of Knots

In the eighteenth century, improvements in sailing ships allowed different cultures to meet. In 1783, the British ship *Antelope* was wrecked off the coast of Palau and the crew were given refuge by the Palau island king, Abba Thule. After three months, the visitors finished builing a new boat to get them home. The king asked the British sailors if they would take his son, Prince Lee Boo (image at right), with them for his education. While aboard the ship, Lee Boo fascinated the crew with his knot-tying skills.

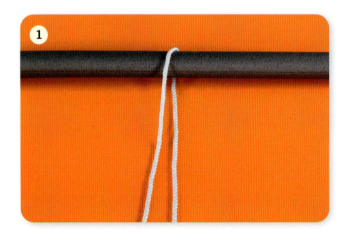

1

Place the working end over the attachment point (which may be a ring or rail, for example) rather than a round turn.

2

Lead the working end over the standing part to the left and under to the right.

DID YOU KNOW? Prince Lee Boo used knots to keep a diary, measuring time and events.

Many ship riggers use the buntline hitch when working with sails because it is sturdy and secure.

A large, fully rigged ship needs a minimum crew of about 30 sailors.

3

The working end now goes up toward the attachment point and over and under the standing part; this forms a second half hitch between the first half hitch and the attachment point.

4

Tighten the knot and slide up to the attachment point.

Clove Hitch

This ancient knot is also known as a mid-line knot. It's used primarily to attach another rope to a post. An easy knot to tie, the clove hitch is often used in sailing and in rock climbing for securing rappelling ropes to an anchor. It is easily adjustable and can be used to tie objects together in a line. This hitch is also useful for creating a temporary sling for an injured arm.

Head for the Heights

There are several essential knots that a climber should know, including the Prusik knot (see page 74) for attaching to fixed ropes, the tensionless hitch (see page 78) for extra security, and the clove hitch for tying in the middle of the a rope and looped on to a carabiner. When you're working your way up the side of a mountain, your life can depend on knowing and tying a quality knot. As always, make sure you understand which knots to use and check that they are secure before trusting them to hold.

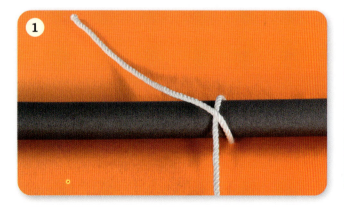

To Tie Around a Rail
The working end goes over and under the rail to the right and then over the standing part to the left.

Take the working end over the rail again and lead it back under the rail and underneath itself. The standing part and working end will be side by side in parallel, but point in opposite directions.

1

To Tie in Hand
Use this method to drop the knot directly over a post. Start as if to make an overhand knot.

2

Now make a second loop, as shown.

3

Place the second loop behind the first loop and the knot is ready to be placed over a post.

This hitch is commonly used in mountaineering for fixing a climber's rope to a carabiner or anchor.

DID YOU KNOW? The clove hitch has been used as a sailing knot for at least 500 years.

Cow Hitch

This knot probably gets its name because it was used to tether a cow to a post so it can graze. It's a quick and easy knot to learn, and it's reliable as long as both ends hold the weight.

Cowboy Knots

Ranchers use a range of knots for herding cattle and roping individual animals. Cowboys use a honda knot, also called a lasso knot or lariat knot, which can be thrown from horseback to catch a cow—or sometimes a wild horse. The honda knot is based on the bowstring knot (see page 98). These days, a rancher's skill with a lasso can be seen during rodeos.

Other knots used by cowboys are the double slipped sheet bend (see page 34), used to tie a horse to a rail, and a reef knot (see page 120) for securing loads to a saddle.

The cow hitch is commonly used to attach luggage tags, which often come with a pre-tied loop of elastic.

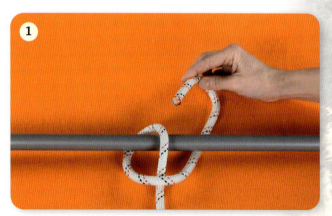

1 Take the working end around to the left, back over the standing part and under the rail to the right.

2 Bring the working end forward over the rail and down under itself to complete the knot. This completes the cow hitch.

DID YOU KNOW? Lassos have been used for millennia. A 3,300-year-old relief carving at the Egyptian temple of Pharaoh Seti I shows the pharaoh lassoing a bull.

Cowboys know how to tie many knots for ranching work. Many of the techniques used on cattle also apply to horses.

3

To secure, pull the short end behind the long end, over the top of the bight (through which the ends go), passing under both of the parts encircling the rail. Work tight.

Highwayman's Hitch

This hitch is often referred to as a "fast getaway" knot for its quick release action. It gets its name from the word *highwaymen*—a term used in the seventeenth century to describe lawless hooligans who overtook stagecoaches and carriages on the open road, and robbed travelers. After the robbery, the highwaymen took off as quickly as possible to avoid capture.

Quick and Convenient

The highwayman's hitch provides a secure fastening to a rail, and it comes loose with a quick tug on the end. It's perfect as a temporary way to hold an object in place, which is why many people use it to secure canoes or kayaks to a dock. This knot is sometimes called a "third hand" for its use as a placeholder when your other two hands are occupied.

Use this knot as a "third hand" in your handicrafts.

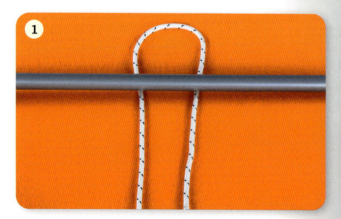

1 Make a bight in the rope and, with the end to the right, place the bight behind the rail to which it is to be attached.

2 Lead the standing part of the rope over and behind this first bight. Bring the standing part down in front of the rail to the left of the rope's working end.

Use a highwayman's hitch to temporarily secure a kayak to the dock while getting into it.

3

Finally, make another bight in the end of the rope and pass this bight through the first bight from the front of the rail, passing over the standing part. The completed knot is shown loose for clarity and needs to be properly drawn up before any load is applied. To release the knot, pull on the working end sharply and it will come away cleanly.

DID YOU KNOW? Legend has it that highwaymen of the Wild West used this hitch to secure their horses while robbing banks.

Gnat Hitch

The gnat hitch is a relatively new knot—it was first documented in 2012. It does a similar job to the buntline hitch (see page 54), but it is easier to tie. It's also easy to release. It has good grip and is jam-resistant unless it is pulled very tight. It is perfect for hanging small objects, such as ornaments or decorations.

Tying the Knot

Although the gnat hitch is new, the use of small knots to represent the joining of two people as a couple is an ageless tradition. That's why the phrase "tying the knot" refers to marriage. The true lovers' knot is usually shown as a pair of overhand knots (see page 12) linked together to join parallel cords in a symmetrical pattern, representing a union. Other true lovers' knots include the carrick bend (see page 26) and the fisherman's knot (see page 28).

The gnat hitch has another garden use—to hang up shiny objects to scare away birds from the berries and seeds.

1 Lead the rope over the attachment point and tie a half hitch around the standing part as shown.

2 Lead the working end to the left behind the standing part.

DID YOU KNOW? The gnat hitch takes its name from the flying insect found in many parts of the world. The gnat and the knot are both small and delicate.

The gnat hitch is used by gardeners to attach string to canes or to hang a bird feeder from a branch.

3
Now tuck the working end down through the loop to the left of the standing part.

4
Tighten the knot, then pull on the standing part to slide the knot up against the attachment point. The completed knot is small and neat.

Ground Line Hitch

This is a neat and simple little hitch for attaching a rope to a rail, pole, or a thicker rope at right angles. Fishermen use it to attach nets and lobster pots to the main rope. When used as a hitch for attaching the end of a rope to a rail or pole, it is better than the clove hitch (see page 56), as it is more secure and less likely to jam. However, it will only work if the pole is cylindrical.

Fishers' Friends

As well as the knots associated with sailing and angling (see page 88), there are other specific knots used by fishers and boaters. These include the killick hitch and slingstone hitch, once used to attach a large stone to rope to act as an anchor for lobster, crab, or eel pots. The killick hitch is a half hitch (see page 44) and a timber hitch (see page 80) used together.

Interestingly, there is a hitch called the lobster buoy hitch, which is similar to the buntline hitch (see page 54). Despite its name, this hitch seems not to be used to attach buoys to lobster pots at all! Instead, it is more useful for tying a rope to a wooden rod.

The ground line hitch is a good knot for hanging up boat fenders.

DID YOU KNOW? The ground line hitch can also be used as a miller's knot to tie a rope around a sack of grain or flour to close it.

Fishers use the ground line hitch to attach crab and lobster pots to a line.

1 Take the working end to the right around the rail or rope to which it is to be attached.

2 Lead the working end to the left over the standing part, around the rail and back over itself. Tuck the working end under the standing part and tighten.

65

Pipe Hitch

Like its name suggests, the pipe hitch is used to pull, lift, and lower a cylindrical pole, such as for scaffolding in construction. It can also be used to attach a rope to a pole where the pull is along the length of the pole.

This knot can be used with a rope to pull a pipe or a spar out of the ground. It can also hoist a pipe, a beam, or roof rafters.

Construction Before the Construction

Before construction workers can start a project, they need to build scaffolding: a temporary support structure, often with multiple floors, that allows workers to access the various levels of the building they are working on. There are many types of scaffolding, some of which even have a type of elevator, called a pulley, which is used to transport materials safely from floor to floor. Most construction scaffolding is made from steel poles, sheets, and bars for their durability. Construction workers use a variety of other knots, loops, and hitches—such as the knute hitch (see page 68)—for various tasks, such as hanging tools and holding buckets.

1. With the working end of the rope, make at least four tight wraps around the pole away from the direction of pull.

2. Take the working end back to the standing part and tie two half hitches (see page 44) around the standing part at the point where the first wrap starts.

When using a pipe hitch to move a pole, pull from the end of the rope, not the wrapped coils.

DID YOU KNOW? The manufacturing of stainless steel pipes is a complex process that uses big machines in giant factories to heat, cool, drill, and straighten the heavy pipes.

67

Knute Hitch

This simple hitch is a good one to know. It is used to attach a cord to a tool or anything with a hole in the handle. Attached in seconds and released just as quickly, this very handy hitch is ideal for hanging a lot of different objects.

Tools of the Trade

Construction workers, electricians, plumbers, and just about every other tradesperson who wears a toolbelt is probably familiar with the knute hitch—even if they aren't familiar with the name. This handy hitch is frequently used to attach tools to the belt itself or to the person while the tool is in use.

Sailors tending to rigging—the system of ropes and chains supporting a ship's mast and sails—also wore a belt with tools. One of these included a marlinspike: a long metal pin used to splice or separate the individual strands of a rope and to loosen tight knots.

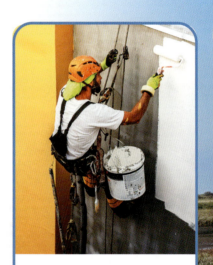

The knute hitch is tied to the paint roller handle and is attached around the painter's wrist so the roller will not fall to the ground if dropped.

Tie a figure 8 knot in the end of a piece of cord. The doubled cord must be able to fit through the hole in the handle, but if the hole is big, place a washer on the cord end before tying the figure 8. The illustrations show a washer being used because the hole is too big.

Make a bight below the figure 8 knot and push the bight through the hole in the handle.

This hitch is particularly useful when attaching rope to a tarp or anything else with eyelets.

3 Bring the figure 8 knot (and washer if used) either around the side of the handle or over the top and through the protruding bight.

4 Pull tight. To remove the cord, loosen the knot and push the figure 8 back through the bight.

DID YOU KNOW? The word *knute* comes from the Old Norse word "knútr," which means "knot."

Marlinspike Hitch

This simple hitch took its name from a marlinspike: a tool used by sailors for working with ropes. This hitch is used to attach a hammer or other tool to a cord or rope in order to make a handle. It is also a good choice of knot to tie around wooden rungs to make a rope ladder.

A Knot of Knowledge

Knots were valuable assets aboard ships, and wise sailors did not just give away their knot knowledge. Sailors traded knot-tying skills, with the most complicated only passed on with a promise to keep them secret. Sailors who could display the most excellent knots were held in high esteem by their crewmates. Sometimes sailors demonstrated their skills by creating decorative knots.

These sea cadets from 1943 are learning how to tie knots and splice rope.

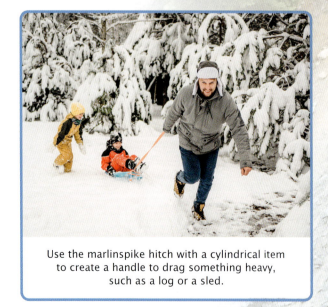

Use the marlinspike hitch with a cylindrical item to create a handle to drag something heavy, such as a log or a sled.

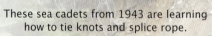

1

Form an overhand loop in the cord.

DID YOU KNOW? At sea, one knot equals one nautical mile per hour, which is the equivalent of 1.85km/h (1.25 mph).

The marlinspike hitch can be used for attaching rungs to a line to make a rope ladder.

Caution must be taken when using this hitch for a rope ladder. Rungs can slide sideways out of the knot.

2

Holding the loop at the point where the rope crosses itself, fold the loop to the left over the left–hand standing part.

3

Insert the bar, hammer, or other tool underneath the middle part going over both sides of the loop. Pull in the direction of the overhand knot. In this example, this will be to the right.

Pile Hitch and Double Pile Hitch

This hitch is easy to tie, yet secure, and is often used to moor boats. The hitch is created in the middle of the rope, so it's a handy knot if the ends of the rope are out of reach or inaccessible. The pile hitch is not possible where the end of whatever it is being tied to is not accessible, such as a floor-to-ceiling pole. And if the line is slippery, use a double pile hitch instead.

Canal Living

Narrowboats are flat-bottomed vessels used for carrying people and cargo along canals. They are similar to barges, which have been used since at least Roman times when they carried wine and olive oil across Europe. Narrowboats were much used in Britain during the Industrial Revolution to carry coal and goods along waterways. Because they are slim and have flat hulls, they can navigate shallow water and the locks that raise or lower the water level. The first narrowboats did not have engines but were pulled along by large shire horses, walking along the canal towpath. Narrowboats are often beautifully painted.

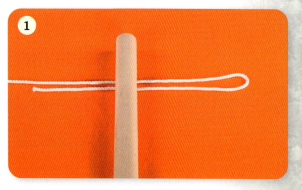

1

Make a bight in the rope and place it alongside the post or rail.

2

Wrap the bight around the post spiraling away from the end of the post or bar.

DID YOU KNOW? Piles are trimmed tree trunks driven into wet ground. They can provide the foundation for buildings, piers, and mooring posts.

The pile hitch can be tied in the middle of a rope.

The pile hitch can be used as a temporary boat mooring becasue it is easy to cast on and off.

3

Now lift the end loop and lift it over the wraps and then over the end of the post. Tighten the knot.

4

To Tie a Double Pile Hitch
Now lift the end loop and lift it over the wraps and then over the end of the post. Tighten the knot.

Prusik Knot

In 1931, Dr. Karl Prusik, a mountaineer from Austria, demonstrated the Prusik knot. It is used to tie a loop of cord, also known as a sling, around a vertical rope. The knot can slide up and down easily, but it locks in place when bearing weight. The useful properties of this knot were instantly recognized and it has become common in sports, such as rock climbing and caving.

As well as a knot, Karl Prusik has a peak in Washington, USA named after him.

Getting Down Fast

Rappelling, also called abseiling, is using ropes to make a controlled descent from a height. Early rappelling was done with the user wrapping the rope around the body. This created friction with the rope, which slowed the descent, but it could be hard to control and also result in rope burns. The use of a double rope and a device called a descender has made this sport much easier. It's also made pausing on the way down possible. Many descenders feature self-locking devices that grip the rope if the climber appears to be dropping too fast.

Climbers can use a mechanical version of the Prusik knot to help them climb up ropes. The device, called an ascender, grips on to a vertical rope and enables a climber to move upward even with a heavy backpack.

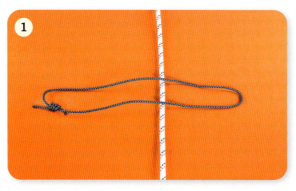

Place a bight of the sling across the main rope.

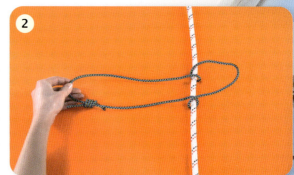

Lead the bight under the main rope and tuck the remainder of the sling down through this bight.

DID YOU KNOW? Rock climbing emerged as a sport from Alpine mountaineering in the late nineteenth century.

The Prusik knot is useful for making a rope "handle" on a vertical rope.

When used to create a handle, this knot can hold a bucket from a suspension line.

3

Now take the bight down under the main rope and around again in the centre between the first wraps. Again tuck the remainder of the sling down through the bight. (If the rope is icy or slippery, a third turn can be taken, making a double Prusik.)

4

Work the coils tight, making sure that they are parallel and not crossed – the main loop of the sling must emerge from the middle of the wraps.

Rolling Hitch

The rolling hitch can be used to attach a rope to a smooth vertical scaffolding pole. This hitch can be slid along the pole by hand to adjust its position, but it will grip when pulled tightly. It's useful in moving heavy loads along a line, and it can also be used to attach one rope to another.

On a Roll

This hitch is used for a number of purposes, from construction and camping to sailing and scaffolding. It has a strong grip, and it doesn't take long to untie. It won't, however, grip to a slippery line or a rope with a small diameter.

The rolling hitch can be use by a scaffolder or roof worker to raise a tool or pipe from the ground.

To Tie Over a Rope
Use this method to tie to another rope.

1

As with a solid pole, use the working end to make at least two wraps but this time trapping the standing part, as shown, and working away from the direction of pull.

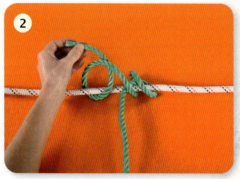

2

With the working end, tie a half hitch around the pole.

3

Work the knot tight by pulling on both the working end and the standing parts.

76

To Tie Over a Pole
Use this method to tie to a pole.

1

2

With the working end, make at least two complete wraps around the pole in the direction of the pull. Add more wraps if the surface or rope is slippery or slick.

Take the working end back over the pole and the wraps, and tie a half hitch to the left of the standing part. Work tight before loading.

For heavier loads, create more friction by adding more wraps to the hitch.

DID YOU KNOW? Archeological evidence shows that various scaffolding systems have been in use since prehistoric times.

Tensionless Hitch

This knot is often used in rescue situations, but it can be useful for tasks, such as hanging a monkey swing (a flat disk with a rope through the middle) from the branch of a tree. This hitch is simple to tie, but it should be used in conjuction with a large shackle or a carabiner.

Serious About Safety

This hitch is often used in rescue operations because it is strong and secure—in fact, it's one of the strongest hitches for securing weight-bearing loads. In a rescue from the top of a cliff or a mountain, for example, this hitch will be fastened to a sturdy tree branch to support the backboard or crate holding the person or animal being rescued.

It's another useful hitch for construction or other utility purposes, as well, such as supporting workers or window washers rappelling the side of a building.

The tensionless hitch is used for heavy–duty purposes.

Make a small loop (an eye) in the working end of the rope. A figure 8 Loop or an angler's loop is recommended.

With the working end, make several wraps around the tree limb or other support pole—the number of wraps will depend on the strain on the rope and how rough or smooth the tree limb is (a minimum of three wraps and as many as five may be needed). Once it's wrapped, pulling the standing part should not cause the wraps to slip, so add more as needed.

DID YOU KNOW? The tensionless hitch is ideal for attaching a swing to a strong branch of a tree. Use a figure 8 knot as a stopper under the swing seat.

The rescue line can be secured at the top with the tensionless hitch as it is very strong and secure.

Carabiners are an essential part of the climber's kit. These clips feature a spring–loaded gate to trap a loop of rope. They are also very handy for hooking tools on to belts and backpacks.

3

Attach a shackle or carabiner to the eye of the working end and around the main standing part. This acts as a fail–safe just in case something should go wrong.

Timber Hitch

This handy, secure hitch is easy to make, simple to undo, and does not jam. It's called a timber hitch because it was devised for the purpose of pulling large logs. It is also used to attach strings on some stringed instruments, such as the guitar and the ukulele.

Treetop Knot

The timber hitch is an ancient knot and was first descibed in a nautical instruction booklet from 1625. Today, it is highly valued by arborists (people who look after individual trees) because it works well on cylindrical objects such as tree branches. Unlike other knots, this can also be fastened in a metal chain, which is useful when greater strength is needed.

The timber hitch is used to attach ukulele or classical guitar strings to the bridge.

Lead the working end around the log, then over the standing part and under the loop just formed.

Now wrap the working end around the leg of the loop, so that the standing part runs through a small eye, making a noose. Be careful to wrap around the loop leg, which was made by the working end. If using laid rope, or rope strands twisted into spirals, wrap the rope in the same direction as the lay so it fits alongside neatly.

DID YOU KNOW? A "knot" in a plank of wood is an irregularity in the ggrain. It is formed when a tree loses a branch and the tree continues growing around it.

Use this hitch when pruning trees. Attach a rope to the branch you want to prune. Once tied, lead the rope over a higher branch and tether to a solid object on the ground.

Cut branches can be lowered safely by releasing tension on the rope.

3

When the standing part is pulled, the noose will tighten and the wraps will be trapped against the log. Following these steps without tying it round anything will produce a free-standing noose.

4

Adding a Killick Hitch
Take the standing part of the rope toward the end of the log in the direction it is to be pulled, and place a half hitch around the log itself. Adjust the half hitch, so that when the standing part is pulled, the half hitch grips the log near to the end, but not so close that it slips off.

Chapter 4

Loop Knots

This chapter covers adjustable and fixed-size loops, which can be used for a variety of purposes—everything from fishing and climbing to search and rescue operations. But not all loops have practical purposes. The endless, or eternal, knot is purely decorative and is an important symbol in many cultures, including Celtic, Islamic, and Chinese traditions.

Getting Hitched

Here's a quick look at the loop knots in this chapter.

Overhand Loop: Attaches to hooks and clips, and can be used as a stopper knot.

Figure 8 Loop: A common loop used by cavers.

Angler's Loop: Used most commonly in fishing.

Common Bowline: Frequently used in rescue operations to lower people to safety.

Bowline on a Bight: Used for climbing and for making a temporary harness.

Double Bowline: Most useful when using wet, stiff, or slippery rope.

Water Bowline: Used in situations involving water because it's easy to untie.

Bowstring Knot: An ancient knot used in archery.

Butterfly Loop: Often used in caving and climbing.

Reverse Bowline: Useful for mooring a large boat or when you need a large loop.

Lanyard Knot: An easy little knot for attaching badges or making a zip pull.

Farmer's Loop: Often used to make a handle or for hanging items.

Poacher's Knot: Used to make a handle or tie down a tarp without eyelets.

A Chinese medallion featuring an endless knot design.

Overhand Loop

This simple but secure loop is quick and easy to tie, but it's difficult to undo once it's been pulled tight. It can be used to attach hooks, clips, and other ropes to a line, or tied near to the end of a line to form a reliable stopper knot. Like the overhand knot, the overhand loop is often used in conjunction with other knots and should not be relied upon to hold super heavy loads.

Ready-made Loops

Loops aren't just for cords and ropes! Many yarn handcrafts, such as knitting and crocheting, are almost entirely dependent on making loops to hold stitches in place. Most projects start with at least a single loop and progress from there using a series of over, under, and through stitches to create a desired pattern. Some crafters like to get hands-on—giant loop yarn is created specifically for those who prefer to knit with their fingers instead of needles.

An overhand loop is handy for hanging tools—and even bundles of ropes—from a horizontal pole.

Double-up the cord to make a bight. Tie an overhand knot (see page 12) in the doubled cord, so that the bight emerges to form a loop at the end.

DID YOU KNOW? Like rope, yarn is made from both natural and synthetic materials. The best quality yarns are usually made from animal fibers, such as angora (from rabbits) and cashmere (from goats).

Loop yarn comes in many different colors and sizes. It's ideal for knitting using your hands instead of knitting needles.

2

Tighten by pulling the loop away from the doubled cord.

Figure 8 Loop

The figure 8 loop is tied the same way as the figure 8 knot (see page 14), but using a doubled cord. There are two ways of tying this loop—use whichever you find easiest.

Below Ground

The figure 8 loop is one commonly used by cavers, along with the bowline and the butterfly loop (see page 100). While some caves can be walked or crawled into from ground level, others require the use of ropes. Caving is not for the faint-hearted. It can involve squeezing through tight passages, crossing deep gaps, and wading through deep water. Hard hats should be worn in case of bumps or falling rocks and should have an attached light to show the way in the dark. A back-up light should also be carried, along with a first-aid kit, water, and emergency food rations.

The figure 8 loop is the standard method for tying a rope to a climbing harness.

1 Double-up the cord to create a bight, then fold the bight over the doubled standing part as shown. This is tied in the same way as a single line figure 8 knot but using the doubled line.

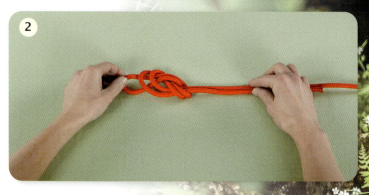

2 Wrap the bight under the doubled standing part, and back through the loop formed by the doubled cord.

Some caves need special equipment to enter. Cavers can be lowered in from above or rappel down the side.

Regularly visited caves may feature fixed ropes for cavers to follow. These ropes are already anchored into the rocks.

3

ALTERNATIVE METHOD
Start with a simple, single-line figure 8 knot. With the working end, retrace the knot, keeping the cords side by side, to form the loop.

DID YOU KNOW? The deepest known cave on Earth is Veryovkina Cave in the country of Georgia. It descends to 2,209 m (7,247 ft).

Angler's Loop

Also known as the perfection loop, this is an old fishing knot that can be used with modern synthetic line. It is secure, but it can jam if it is tied tightly, so only use it when untying is not needed. There are two methods of tying this loop. Method 1 is for occasions when you need a loop at the end of a cord. Method 2 can be used to make the loop around an object or through a ring.

Knotty Fish

Anglers need to know knots to attach their lines to a reel, join lines, and tie on a hook, but there is also a fish familiar with knots. The hagfish is an eel-like jawless fish that scavenges on the seabed, feeding on carcasses from the inside out. If it struggles to gnaw its way through the skin of a whale, it has a neat trick—tying itself into a knot! The hagfish creates a simple overhand knot with its body and uses it as leverage to push its head deeper into the carcass. Hagfish secrete slime, so they can wriggle back out of the knot with ease. The slime also makes them taste unpleasant.

1

Method 1
Make a bight in the rope with the working end to the left. Take the working end under the standing part and back over the bight to form a larger loop to the right.

2

Take the working end and wrap it around the top of the original bight.

3

Take the larger loop from the right and pass it up through the front of the original bight. Pull the loop and both ends to tighten the knot.

1

2

3

Method 2
Make a simple overhand knot (see page 12) in the rope at the point where the final knot is needed. Note that this knot is formed by going under first, then over.

Feed the working end through the object that will be attached to loop (such as a ring), and work back through the loop of the overhand knot, making a slip knot.

Lead the working end underneath the hanging part, and squeeze it through the overhand knot, as shown. Finally, feed the working end underneath itself, as shown. Pull the loop and hanging part of the rope to tighten the knot.

This loop works well with standard string or cord, and also with stretchy cord—unlike most loop knots.

DID YOU KNOW? The angler's loop is secure for use with stretchy rope or bungee cord for use on a trailer.

Common Bowline

Also known simply as the bowline, pronounced "bo-lin," this knot is simple to tie and won't jam. It is easy to untie, as long as it is not tied to a load. The common bowline can become loose, so for more secure versions, the double bowline (see page 94) and the water bowline (see page 96) are good alternatives.

King of Knots

If there had to be a list of the top three knots, the bowline would stand alongside the sheet bend (see page 32) and the clove hitch (see page 56). The bowline is known as the "king of knots" for its importance and long history. It has been used at sea for hundreds of years and can be used for multiple purposes. This knot may have been described in the book *The Sea-Mans Grammar*, written by the English explorer Captain John Smith in 1627. He wrote, "The boling knot is also so firmly made and fastened by the bridles into the cringles of the sails, they will break, or the sail split before it will slip."

Two bowlines can be used to join two separate ropes.

1

Make a small loop, as shown.

DID YOU KNOW? A bowline knot has been found in the rigging of a buried ship belonging to the ancient Egyptian pharaoh Khufu.

The bowline is used during rescue operations, saving people who have fallen down a hole or need lowering from a height.

2

Take the working end up and pass it through the small loop formed in Step 1, then down behind the standing part.

3

Bring the working end back down through the small loop, following the same path as before. Tighten the knot carefully, keeping the working end inside the larger loop.

Bowline on a Bight

This knot has two independent loops. When both standing parts are loaded, it creates a closed system that will not slip. It is useful where two separate anchor points are required, or where a line has to be split into two at an attachment point. It can be tied without needing access to the rope ends.

To Tie Without the Ends

First make a long bight in the rope. Using the doubled rope, make an overhand loop (see page 84) as if starting a bowline with the doubled rope. Bring the end loop up through this overhand loop.

To tighten take hold of the two strands around the base of this loop and pull them out to form a double loop. Be careful not to make a slip loop by pulling out the wrong part. Once tightened, this is a secure double loop.

Now take the end loop, open it up and take it back over the knot.

DID YOU KNOW? The bowline on a bight knot can be used to create a foothold in a rope.

The bowline on a bight allows a load to be split across two anchor points for extra safety.

If modern equipment is not available, the bowline on a bight can be used as a temporary climbing harness, by placing one leg in each of the loops.

To Tie Using One End
Start by tying a loose common bowline (see page 90), but make sure that the working end is much longer than usual. Take the working end parallel to the leg of the loop next to it and follow this around the original knot.

1

2

Continue following the knot round until the working end emerges alongside the standing part.

Double Bowline

This knot, also called the round turn bowline, is more secure than the common bowline (see page 90), and it is easy to tie. It has what is known as a double nipping loop, which provides more grip when working with stiff or slippery material.

Mariner's Log Line

Knots are not just for securing objects, but also used for measuring. A log line was a way of gauging the speed of a ship before modern instruments. It consisted of a spool wound with a long rope that had a knot tied every seven fathoms (about 13 m, or 42 ft). At the end of the rope was the "log," a flat piece of wood that dragged in the water. This log was thrown overboard from the rear of the ship. As the ship sailed, the knotted rope unwound from the spool. A sailor then counted the number of knots that passed over the ship's rail in 30 seconds. Dividing the number of knots and length of rope by the time, the sailor was able to calculate the rough speed of the ship. This is how knots came to be used as a measure for ship speed.

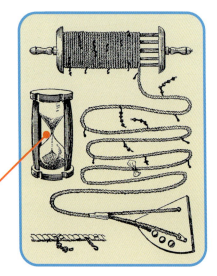

Sailors used an hourglass to measure the log line time accurately.

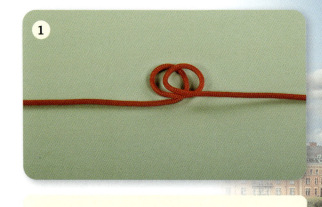

1

Start by making two overhand loops (see page 84), one on top of the other, like this.

2

Take the working end underneath and then through the middle of the loops made in Step 1.

DID YOU KNOW? Ship captains recorded their ship's progress in a "logbook" named after the log used with a log line.

The double bowline is commonly used in climbing to attach a rope to a fixed object, such as a tree.

The double bowline, which provides a little more security than the common bowline, is often used on a mooring rope.

3

Now pass the working end underneath the standing part and back through the middle of the two loops, ending up inside the large loop on the right. Tighten carefully by pulling on both ends and the main loop.

Water Bowline

The water bowline is so called because even after it has been in water, it is still easy to undo. This is another knot that offers more security than the common bowline.

Knot in Water

There are many watersports, such as kayaking, sailing, boating, canoeing, and rafting, that require the use of knots. In waterskiing, wakeboarding, and tubing, knots are also used to connect a rope to the watercraft on one end and to the equipment on the other end. Loops are also used to secure the surfboard to the surfer.

Many water sports use synthetic ropes, such as those made from polypropylene. They are manufactured in a huge range of colors so they can easily be identified for their strength and purpose.

The water bowline is fairly easy to tie, even with wet hands or when wearing gloves.

Make two overhand loops (page 84). Slide the second loop under the first to form a clove hitch (page 56).

Take the working end up and pass it through the small loops formed in Step 1, then down behind the standing part.

DID YOU KNOW? Some special forces, such as the elite US Navy SEALs, are required to master underwater knot tying as part of their training.

The water bowline is ideal in wet conditions, such as where a rope will be submerged in water, as it is less prone to slipping or jamming.

3

Thread the working end back through both loops.

4

Carefully tighten the knot.
NOTE: Under load the two loops of the clove hitch may separate. This is to be expected and does not mean that the knot is slipping.

Bowstring Knot

The bowstring knot is one of the simplest and also one of the oldest knots known. As the name suggests, it can be used with wooden bow and arrow sets. It's quick, simple to tie, and secure.

Sign of Solomon

In medieval times, archers were familiar with the knots used on their bows. They may have also recognized Solomon's knot: a decorative motif found in Roman mosaics and ancient synagogues, and adopted as a Christian symbol in churches across Europe. This knot represents unity and eternity. It is named for the biblical king Solomon, who was said to have been given a powerful signet ring by an angel which featured a knot.

In Christianity, Solomon's knot is said to symbolize the bond between people and God.

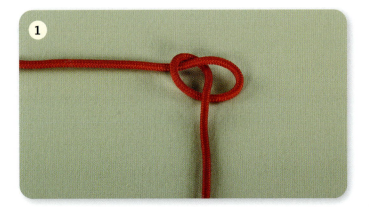

1

Tie an overhand knot (see page 14) in the rope, exactly like this. You need to be able to make a loop from the length of rope in the working end, so don't tie the knot too close to the end.

2

Take the working end up and through the middle of the overhand knot, as shown. It is essential that the knot is tied exactly this way—if the end is tucked through the overhand knot any other way, it will slip.

Unlike other loops that tighten when the rope is pulled, the bowstring knot gets bigger. It can be used as a temporary dog collar and leash without harming the animal.

As the name suggests, this knot can be used to attach a bow string to the notch at each tip of a bow.

3

Tighten the overhand knot to trap the working end, forming a loop. This loop can be adjusted easily by pulling on the working end. Surprisingly, the working end does not easily slip if the loop is pulled on, but adding an overhand knot or stopper knot at the end of the working end will prevent it from slipping out completely.

DID YOU KNOW? The oldest evidence for the use of the bow and arrow are arrowheads found at the Sibudu Cave in South Africa from over 60,000 years ago.

Butterfly Loop

Sometimes referred to as the Alpine butterfly—it was published in *The Alpine Journal* in the 1920s—this strong, secure loop ties in the middle of a rope. It will take a load in any direction, and it can easily be tied around the hand and adjusted as it is tied.

Take Up the Slack

This loop is untied easily, which is why it's ideal for taking up slack in rope line. For example, if your rope is too long for its intended purpose, use the butterfly loop. Select the location of the rope line you'd like to shorten, and create the loop. Pull on the loop until the line is positioned in the correct spot.

This loop is perfect for isolating a section of damaged rope. Simply pull the damaged part into the loop, and tie it. This stops putting any more strain on that section of the rope.

1

Make two turns around the hand.

2

Take the rope around again, but this time lay it in between the other two turns.

3

Lift up the turn closest to the fingertips and take it to the left over the other two turns.

DID YOU KNOW? In the seventeenth century, the French king Louis XIV employed a cravatier to select and tie a decorative ribbon around the king's neck each day.

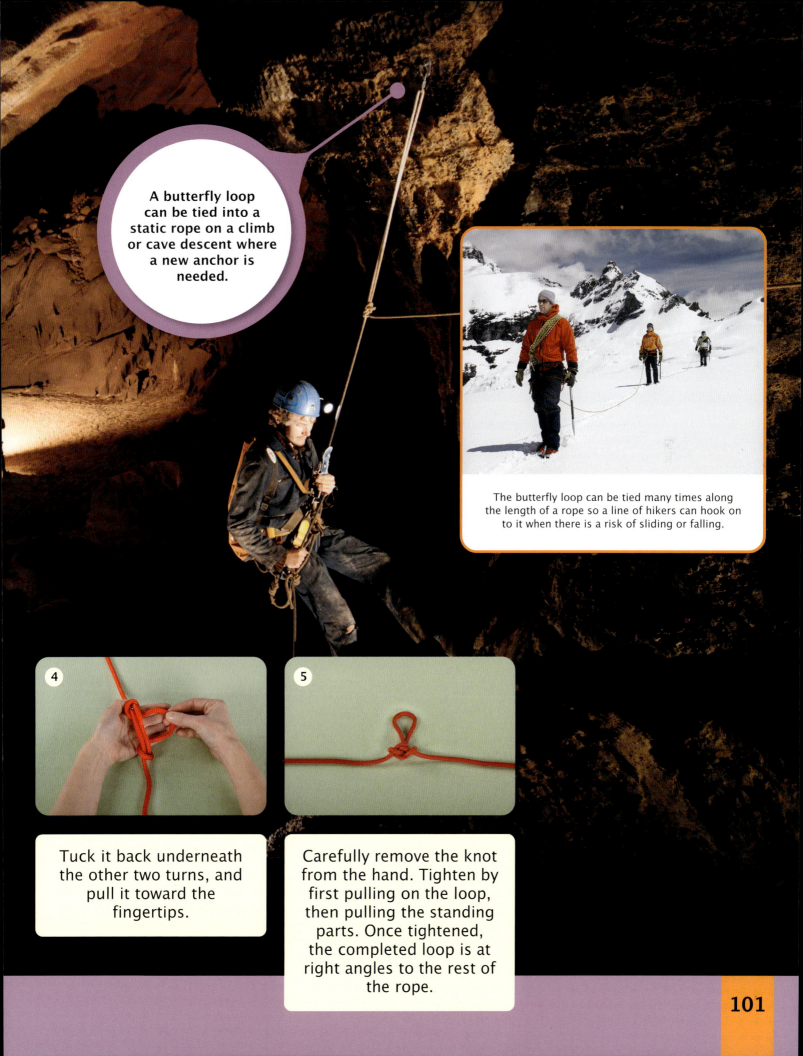

A butterfly loop can be tied into a static rope on a climb or cave descent where a new anchor is needed.

The butterfly loop can be tied many times along the length of a rope so a line of hikers can hook on to it when there is a risk of sliding or falling.

4

Tuck it back underneath the other two turns, and pull it toward the fingertips.

5

Carefully remove the knot from the hand. Tighten by first pulling on the loop, then pulling the standing parts. Once tightened, the completed loop is at right angles to the rest of the rope.

Reverse Bowline

Alternatively known as the "Eskimo" bowline and anti-bowline, this variation of a bowline has been in use by the Inuit people for hundreds of years. Compared to a common bowline, this version can better withstand its loop being pulled outward. It is also easy to turn this into a slipped loop, so that it can be quickly undone.

From the Mouth of Giants

Research into Inuit knots has found examples from over a thousand years ago. Lacking land plants and their fibers for creating ropes, the Inuit used whatever materials they could get their hands on, including sinew, rawhide (leather), deep-sea grass, and baleen. Baleen is the filter system found in the mouth of the Greenland whale. It is made up of bony fringes like a comb. This was shredded into fine strips and tied together to make useful lengths. A benefit of this marine material was that it was waterproof.

Inuit Sled

In 1818, the British polar explorer John Ross brought an Inuit sled back to London. The sled was made from whale and walrus bones and tied together with walrus cord. Its construction was of great interest to the Victorians.

1 Make a small loop in the cord.

2 Take the working end down through the loop.

3 Lead the working end under the standing part and over to the right.

4

Now take the working end back up through the first small loop you made and back out behind the bigger loop, as shown. Make sure you lead the cord over, under, over, under, in that order.

5

Tighten carefully, checking that one face of the knot looks like this.

This bowline is most useful when you need to form a large loop at the end of a rope.

The reverse bowline is used to moor a boat to a large bollard.

DID YOU KNOW? The reverse bowline is known as the Cossack knot in Russia.

Lanyard Knot

This classic loop knot, also known as the friendship or diamond knot, is ideal for making a lanyard and attaching a name badge.

Decorative Knots

The lanyard knot is both practical and decorative. Interesting knots can be appreciated for their appearance and uses. With time on their hands, sailors of old developed their knot-tying skills by creating more elaborate and complex designs, repeating knot patterns. These types of knots can be used as jewelry, mats, handles, or tassels. It is worth adding a few decorative designs to your knot-tying repertoire.

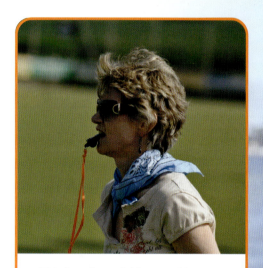

This knot is useful for attaching any items worn loosely around the neck, such as a referee whistle.

1 Start by tying a carrick bend (page 26) but leave it flat as shown. Place the knot over your hand to make it easier.

2 Take the left-hand end down to the right (in the same direction that it is pointing), over the leg of the loop and up through the carrick bend.

3 Now take the right-hand end up to the left, over the leg of the loop and up through the carrick bend alongside the left end. Both should now point in the same direction, away from the main loop.

4

Hold the two ends in one hand and the loop in the other hand and gently work the knot together.

5

The finished knot when fully tightened.

The lanyard knot can be made into a simple zip pull using thin cord.

DID YOU KNOW? During Jewish celebrations, such as Shabbat, a special knotted bread is baked. The challah can be a long loaf made from ropes of dough that are braided, or smaller knotted balls.

Farmer's Loop

This is another loop that can be made in the middle of a rope when you don't have access to the ends. It is easy and quick to tie around the hand. It's a strong and secure loop that follows a memorable sequence of moves.

Farmers' Knots

As its name suggests, this knot was used by farmers, both for practical and for superstitious reasons. It was believed that this knot would ward away the evil that might befall crops and livestock. The farmer's loop and other decorative knots were sometimes hung up outside buildings to ward away evil spirits. In Eastern Europe, these magic knots were thought to seal the mouths of hungry wolves. In sowing season, Indonesian farmers listened for a hoot from an owl, and then tied a knot in a blade of grass. This was then buried in the field where the crops were to be sown, as it captured the promise of a good harvest.

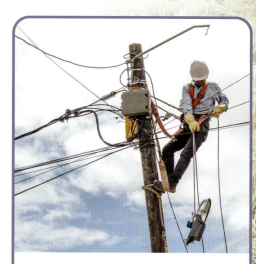

The farmer's loop is useful for making a handhold, hanging tools, or shortening a longer rope.

1. Wrap the rope around your hand three times, so that there are three cord parts side by side.

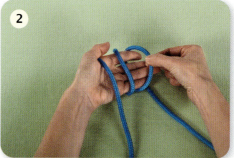

2. Lift the middle cord and move it over to the right.

3. Lift the new middle cord and move it over to the left.

DID YOU KNOW? In Scotland, plaited cords were knotted around the necks of cattle to keep witches away from barns.

Use the farmer's loop to create a loop in the middle of a rope to use as a handle for carrying bundles.

4
Then lift the new middle cord and move it over to the right.

5
Now lift the new middle cord up and away from your palm and slide your hand out of the rest of the cord. Pull on the loop you are holding and tighten the knot beneath it.

6
This is the completed loop.
How to remember the sequence:
middle to right
middle to left
middle to right
middle goes up

Poacher's Knot

The poacher's knot, also referred to as a carabiner knot and scaffold knot, tightens as the object it's attached to pulls on it. It grips well, which is why it's useful with a carabiner or scaffold hooks—**although** it will collapse through on itself unless there is something in the loop to stop it. This knot can be paired with a thimble: a plastic or metal object inserted into the loop to add support and stop it from wearing.

Utility Knot

The poacher's knot and thimble combination can be used for many purposes, including hanging a hammock in conjunction with a becket hitch (see page 50), as well as for hanging heavy tools or other equipment in place. It's ideal for hanging a load from pegs and hooks, and it fares well for climbing trees when used with a carabiner.

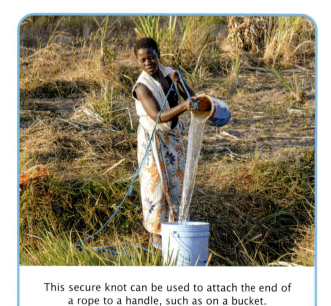

This secure knot can be used to attach the end of a rope to a handle, such as on a bucket.

1

Make a large bight in the working end. Take the working end up and over the standing part, as shown. Wrap the working end back around itself and the main length of rope twice, heading toward the loop. Keep the turns loose at this stage.

2

Thread the working end back through all the turns made in Step 1. Tighten the knot by pulling on the working end.

DID YOU KNOW? The poacher's knot was originally used by poachers to trap small birds and animals.

To hold a tarp down without an eyelet, place a stone under a section of tarp. Slip a poacher's knot around the tarp and stone. Repeat around the tarp where needed.

3

If a thimble is to be used, insert it into the loop, as shown, before tightening. Support the thimble as you tighten the knot, so it doesn't slide out of position. Adjust the loop to the size required by sliding the knot along the length of rope.

Chapter 5

Binding and Other Knots

A binding knot is tied around one or more objects to hold them together. This could be a bundle of sticks, a wrapped parcel, or a roll of carpet. It can also be used to hold a carpentry project, such as a chair frame, together while it is being glued.

In a Bind

Here's a quick glance at the knots in this chapter.

Constrictor Knot: Works on curved surfaces for securing items in place.

Gleipnir: A mulipurpose knot for securing light and heavy loads.

Pole Lashing: Used to bundle sticks or poles together.

Strangle Knot: Used on curved surfaces to secure items in place.

Reef Knot, Reef Knot (Locked): Works to bind cloth. The Locked version secures the ends into the knot.

Cat's Paw: Used to connect rope to hooks and for moving heavy-duty cargo in shipyards.

Binding knots are useful for holding glued objects together while the glue dries.

Constrictor Knot

This binding knot is suitable for curved surfaces. It is ideal for tying around a bundle or to hold some braided cords or other objects together permanently.

Warning: This knot is very difficult to untie and should never be tied around a part of the body!

Two Methods

There are two tying methods. The first is for tying the knot around something large, when you are able to use the working end. The second method is tied in your hand, mid-line, then placed over or around an object.

To Tie Around Something
Loop the working end of your cord over the object, so it hangs to the right of the standing part. Take it left across itself and around the object again, so it hangs down from behind.

To Tie in Hand
Start by folding the cord in an underhand loop.

Pull the left side of the loop down, so the loop lies over the cord.

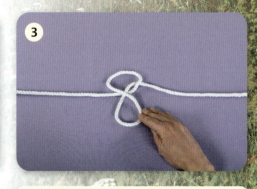

Twist the lower half of the loop to the right to form a figure 8 shape.

DID YOU KNOW? The constrictor knot is often used in human and veterinary surgery for its strength and holding power.

2

Lead the working end up and over the standing part, then thread it beneath the crossed cords at the top of the object. This forms an overhand knot, trapped underneath the wrapped cord.

3

Pull both ends hard to tighten.

This knot is a good choice for tying a bundle of cables, ropes, or poles together.

4

Now fold the lower loop of the figure 8 under and upward, so that the loops are one on top of the other, as shown.

5

Place the two loops around whatever is to be bound, then pull the ends to tighten.

Gleipnir

The gleipnir knot is a simple knot that can form a binding around just about anything. You will need a cord long enough to pass around the object twice, with enough left over to complete the knot. It's ideal for large, bulky items that would be otherwise hard to secure.

The Legend of Fenrir

The word *gleipnir* comes from Norse mythology and refers to the knot used to restrain Fenrir. In Norse legend, Fenrir was a giant wolf prophesized to kill Odin during Ragnarök, the death of the gods. It was decided that Fenrir should be tied up. When he broke free of the first chains a magical iron rope, named Gleipnir, was ordered. The rope was said to contain the sound of a cat's step, the beard of a woman, mountain roots, a bear's sinews, the breath of a fish, and bird spit. Since these were used in the rope, they are no longer found on Earth.

Double the cord and, with a finger in the bight, twist once.

Fold the small loop back on itself and, holding this loop, place the doubled cord around the object or objects to be bound. The loop needs to be positioned close to the left edge of the object.

The gleipnir knot can be used to tie bundles of sticks but, unlike the constrictor knot, it is easy to undo.

3

Take one end of the cord and feed it behind and back through the loop. Feed the other end straight through the loop, so that the two ends now point away from each other.

4

Pull the two ends in opposite directions to tighten the knot and lock it in place.

To Undo the Knot
Find the cord end that passes straight through the middle loop and pull it back through the knot. This will loosen and release the knot.

DID YOU KNOW? The Norse word *gleipnir* has been translated as "the entangled one" or "the deceiver."

Pole Lashing

Pole lashing is a handy way of tying a bundle of sticks, canes, or poles together. It's an easy knot to create, and it's simple to undo later.

A Knot for Luck

Once you've lashed your fence together, you may want to add a knotted charm to the gate to offer luck to visitors. This is a Chinese tradition, and knotted cords are still hung up during festivals today. The lucky charm involves tying a symmetrical pattern from one length of cord. Red cord is most often used, as red is a lucky color in Chinese culture. There is evidence of decorative knots being used in China 4,000 years ago. The tradition may have come about following the use of knots for record-keeping.

This binding knot can be used for building a fence of poles.

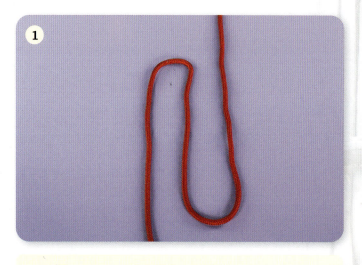

Arrange the cord in a "N" shape, as shown.

Place the bundle of sticks or poles over the middle of the cord, like this.

DID YOU KNOW? Lashing can be used to extend the "length" of a pole by joining poles together toward their ends and tying them in place.

Pole lashing can be used to tie several poles together to form a secure raft.

Poles can also be lashed together to form a cross and even scaffolding.

3

Feed each end through the bight on the opposite side of the bundle and pull the cord tight.

4

Tie the ends in a reef knot (page 120).

Strangle Knot

While its name leaves much to be desired, the strangle knot is not as sinister as it sounds. Like the constrictor knot (see page 112), it is used on a rounded surface, such as a rope or rail. It is also ideal for winding around the end of a rope to stop it fraying. Once tightened, it is difficult to undo and may need to be cut off for removal. Unlike the similar constrictor knot, the ends emerge from the sides of the knot rather than the middle, so it looks neater. **Warning: This knot should never be tied around a part of the body!**

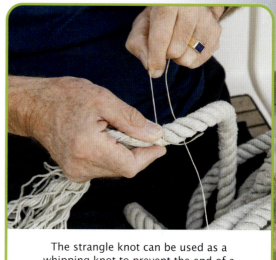

The strangle knot can be used as a whipping knot to prevent the end of a rope from fraying.

Braiding

Braided ropes are preferred by climbers, sailors, and arborists because they do not twist under loads. A braid, or a plait, is made by weaving at least three thick strands of cord together in a repeated order. Numerous patterns are possible with more than three strands. Braiding is also used for styling long hair, of course, as well as in some plumbing pipes.

Braids can also be tied into hair to create extensions.

Pull the rope across the bundle and around it. Pull the working end up and over the first wrap.

The strangle knot creates a binding loop that can be used to tie the neck of a sack.

2

Repeat Step 1 with the working end, following the same path and crossing over the wrap. Push the working end under the first two turns.

3

Pull hard on both ends to tighten.

DID YOU KNOW? Phone charger cables are often bent and tangled during use. Braided cables are more durable than those just coated in plastic.

Reef Knot

The reef knot is a binding knot and can be remembered as "left over right and under, right over left and under." It lies flat once tied and works well binding a roll of cloth or tying shoelaces. To undo, give a sharp tug on one end.

Another Name

The reef knot is also known as a Hercules knot. Hercules was a mythical Roman hero, known for completing 12 impossible tasks. One of these tasks was to steal the girdle (belt) of Hippolyta, the queen of the Amazons. Hippolyta's girdle was tied with a reef knot.

Roman Wedding

The reef knot is an ancient symbol of love and marriage. In Roman weddings, the knot was tied around the bride, and only her groom was allowed to untie it.

The reef knot was worn in ancient Greece and Rome as a protective amulet. The design appears in many items of jewelry, including armbands and belts, as well as ancient Greek mosaic flooring.

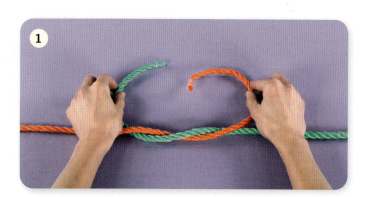

1

Position the two cords like this, with the two working ends loosely wrapping around each other.

2

Now take the working end on the left and lay it over the other working end. Continue to lead the cords as above, so the knot is neat and symmetrical. Pull all ends to tighten.

DID YOU KNOW? It was once thought that the thread stitching together a wound should be tied with a reef knot, and that this would help the injury heal more quickly.

This knot has been used since ancient times to tie belts and sashes. A modern use includes tying the obi (belt) of a martial arts keikogi (uniform).

The reef knot is one of the most important knots for Scouts to learn. It appears on the Scouts' World Membership Badge.

Reef Knot (Locked)

This version of the reef knot locks in the working ends of both ropes. However, it shouldn't be used to join ropes where the material or size of the ropes are different, as the knot may come undone.

The reef knot can be seen in ancient Egyptian carvings among hieroglyphs.

Ancient Knots

The reef knot is one of several knots known and used by the ancient Egyptians. It appears in hieroglyphs and statues, and in one instance it appears to fasten a kilt. Excavations at Berenike, a harbor on the Egyptian Red Sea coast, have unearthed examples of cords and netting from the first century CE, with hundreds of examples of reef knots, overhand knots (see page 12), and figure 8 knots (see page 14).

The tying method can be remembered as "left over right and under, right over left and under."

1 Position the two cords like this, with the two working ends loosely wrapping around each other.

2 Now take the working end on the left and lay it over the other working end. Continue to lead the cords as above, so the knot is neat and symmetrical.

3

Pull all the ends to tighten the knot.

An emergency first-aid sling or a bandage is finished with a reef knot.

DID YOU KNOW? Ancient Egyptian surveyors used a knotted rope to measure parcels of land. Helpers called rope stretchers were employed to keep the rope taut.

Cat's Paw

This knot is used when a rope is placed over a hook so that if the load becomes unbalanced, it will not immediatcly slip to one side. Once removed from the hook, the knot falls apart instantly so it cannot jam. It is used for hauling cargo from ships. When made from a thin cord and hung from a simple hook, it can have a decorative effect.

Artistic Rope Work

In previous centries, sailors made decorative use of short lengths of unwound rope. Ringbolt hitching, also known as cockscombing, was a craft that involved wrapping a ring, pole, or pipe in a series of hitches producing a decorative, plaited cord weave. The rails of many old ships were adorned with such rope work. Ringbolt hitching can be used for practical purposes, such as to cover a boat fender to prevent chaffing or to make a handle grip on a pot, but many were for purely decorative purpose.

1 Make a bight in the middle of the rope and turn the bight back over the standing parts, forming two loops.

2 Twist each of the loops two to three times in opposite directions (placing a finger into each loop is an easy way). The left-hand loop twists clockwise and the right-hand loop counterclockwise. Add more twists if the load is going to be heavy.

This knot is commonly used to hoist heavy loads from ships.

3

Bring the two loops together and place them over the hook. Make sure that the number of twists on each side is the same. Pull on both standing parts to tighten the knot around the hook.

The cat's paw is an excellent knot for connecting a rope to a hook. If one hoop comes loose, the second should hold.

DID YOU KNOW? Persians use a special knot in hand−knotted carpet making, which allows the creation of very intricate designs in the weaving.

Glossary

BACK-UP KNOT
An extra knot added for security, where failure would be especially dangerous.

BEND
A knot for joining two (or more) ropes.

BIGHT
A curve in a rope. If the curve is completely closed it becomes a loop.

BINDING KNOT
A knot tied around a group of objects to hold them together.

BRAIDING
Interweaving several strands of rope to create a pattern. Sometimes referred to as "plaiting."

CABLE
A name generally used for any large rope, although strictly a cable is a rope made up of three strands.

CORD
A line made up of several strands of yarn plaited together. Technically, a cord is less than 10 mm (0.4 inches) in diameter.

EYE
(1) A small loop formed in the end of a rope.
(2) The name for a ring or hole through which rope can be threaded.

FIBER
A strand of thread.

FRAYING
A rope where the separate strands have begun to unravel.

HALF HITCH
A simple knot made by passing the end of a rope around itself, another rope or an object and then through its own loop.

HANGING PART
The end of a rope that isn't used to create a knot, when the rope is suspended from another object. See also Standing part.

HITCH
A knot for attaching a rope to an object (e.g. a ring) or another rope where the two ropes are not being tied together to form one.

JAM
A knot that has jammed is very difficult to untie.

KNOT SECURITY
A knot's resistance to slipping.

KNOT STRENGTH
The strength of the rope once it has been knotted—a knot reduces the original strength of rope.

LANYARD
(1) A short length of line used to tie down objects on a ship.
(2) A cord worn around the neck to hold an object such as a whistle or an identity card.

LEAD
The direction the working end of a cord takes as it goes through a knot.

LINE
A generic name for a rope, cable, or similar. Technically, a line is a rope that has been used for a particular purpose—a clothesline, for example.

LOAD
To place weight on a knot or line.

LOOP
A circle made in a rope by passing the working end either under or over the standing part.

MAKE FAST
To tie a line to an object.

MARLINSPIKE
A metal instrument with a pointed end used to separate rope strands.

MOORING ROPE
The rope used to secure a boat to the shore.

NIP
The part of a rope where the most friction occurs.

NOOSE
A loop that is not of fixed size, and therefore can easily be adjusted.

OVERHAND LOOP
A loop created in a line by placing the working end over the standing part.

PLAITING
See Braiding.

RAIL
A horizontal bar between two posts, used as a barrier.

ROPE
Technically, to be called rope, material must be at least 10 mm (0.4 inches) in diameter. However the term is used loosely to describe any thick cord from about 6 mm (0.2 inches).

ROUND TURN
A turn in which the working end of a rope is passed all the way around a rail, bar, or similar object, bringing it back alongside its standing part as it comes out of the turn.

SAFE WORKING LOAD
The average weight that a rope can take without breaking, taking into account the rope's age, its prior usage, and the knots involved.

SLACK
A rope or part of a rope that has not been pulled tight.

SLING
An unbroken circle of rope or similar material.

STANDING PART
The section or end of a rope that is not actively being used in creating a knot.

STRAND
A component of rope, made from twisting yarn together.

STRAP
A narrow, flat length of cord..

STOPPER KNOT
A knot which creates a thick end on a rope to prevent it from slipping through a hole.

THIMBLE
A metal ring inserted into a rope to prevent it from fraying.

TUCK
The act of passing the working end of a rope either through a loop or under the standing part to hold it in place.

TURN
One pass of a rope around a rail, bar, or similar object.

UNDERHAND LOOP
A loop created in a rope by placing the working end under the standing part.

WHIPPING
The process of wrapping string or similarly narrow cord around the end of a rope to prevent it from fraying.

WORKING END
The end of a rope actively being used to create a knot.

YARN
A line created by twisting together fibers. Yarn is then further plaited to create a line with a larger diameter.

Index